Chinese Women
in Love and Marriage

Other books by Dawn Xiao Yan Li

1. Finding True Love Online, Published by China Youth Press in February 2006

2. Modern Marriage & Lasting Love, published by Asian Promise Ltd. in December 2005

3. Connecting You to Love, published by Hong Kong Cosmos Books in May 2005

Chinese Women in Love and Marriage

A Guide to Happiness in Cross-Cultural Relationships

Dawn Xiao Yan Li

iUniverse, Inc.
New York Lincoln Shanghai

Chinese Women in Love and Marriage
A Guide to Happiness in Cross-Cultural Relationships

iUniverse books may be ordered through booksellers or by contacting:

iUniverse
2021 Pine Lake Road, Suite 100
Lincoln, NE 68512
www.iuniverse.com
1-800-Authors (1-800-288-4677)

ISBN-13: 978-0-595-41506-9 (pbk)
ISBN-13: 978-0-595-85855-2 (ebk)
ISBN-10: 0-595-41506-7 (pbk)
ISBN-10: 0-595-85855-4 (ebk)

Printed in the United States of America

This book is dedicated with deepest love to my husband, Richard Kaser.

Contents

Acknowledgments

I am so lucky to have Scott Merry help me with the editing work. His great life experience, language sense and friendship have brought me confidence to publish my first book in English. I would also like to thank the gentlemen who took part in the Asian Promise email survey at the end of 2004, and all the gentlemen and ladies who have offered valuable information to Asian Promise now and in the past. I have to say the book would not have been possible without their support.

Most of all, my great thanks go to my husband Richard Kaser and to our children. Richard's love and intelligence supported me in many ways—belief, confidence, courage, ideas, technical support, and more. Words are inadequate to express my appreciation to him. Our children Simone and Leo give me important spiritual support. Their unconditional love and kindness has created such a wonderful world in my life. With great love from my family, I am able to help others to achieve love and happiness.

Introduction

In the summer of 2000 I brought my newborn son Leo from Hong Kong to visit my home city of Beijing. My son is a Euro-Asian boy (my husband is English) born in the first year of my third marriage. Many friends and family members were curious and came to see Leo and me. The curiosity of family and friends soon turned into admiration. And why not? A lady once divorced and once widowed, now 40 with a 10 year-old daughter from the first marriage, had remarried and had a new happy family again, which all sounded too mythical to Chinese people. But seeing is believing. I had so many reasons for Chinese women to admire me. However my delighted heart soon sank as their reaction changed from admiration to longing for help in their own situations.

I left China in 1991 and the country has changed immensely since then. Enormous changes on the economic side have been matched by those in personal life, greatly challenging the Chinese attitudes to love and marriage. The divorce rate has risen from 0.07% in 1980 to 20% in 2005, and the trend is still going up. Around 80% of those divorced are 30-50 years of age. Many of my friends are also in this age group, have a child, and are either already divorced or on the way.

Now Chinese people have begun to look for true love and quality marriage. Although the single, lifelong marriage of the past has become history, there remain some old Chinese thoughts from thousands of years of tradition that are still deeply rooted. Unfortunately, Chinese women suffer greatly from the effects of those old thoughts. Chinese men can easily have a second marriage at any age, but this is not the case for women, particularly for divorced women, and even more so for those with children. Chinese men do not want previously married women, and are not willing to accept their children as his own. The majority of Chinese men still pride themselves on having a beautiful, young and even virgin girlfriend or wife, while values and personality are not as important.

My friends and friends' friends are intelligent and well educated. They are loving, capable and mature, but they cannot find love and have a happy marriage again. They long for it and they deserve to love and to be loved. They value family life so much that they do not mind leaving their own country, giving up their well-paid jobs, or meeting the challenges of a new culture—as long as they can find love again. To them, love is more important than either money or moving to a first world country.

Returning home from my visit with the impression of peoples' reactions etched in my mind, I recounted my experiences, feelings and thoughts to my husband. We both came up with the determination to help Chinese ladies find their love in the world. Through our own experience and that of others we knew in Hong Kong, we knew love was not constrained by national borders and we believed Chinese ladies who could not find love in China, including those previously married, could find love outside of China. The internet has made our dream come true.

Our company Asian Promise has been operating for six years now, and we have helped hundreds of people find love throughout the world. I have written two books in Chinese based on our work experience from Asian Promise. I published my first book, "Connecting You to Love/ Finding True Love Online", in Hong Kong and in mainland China in 2005 and 2006. The book aims to help Chinese people understand and approach the Western idea of love and marriage, viewed from their own background of the traditional Chinese values of love and marriage.

Indeed it is not enough, particularly in cross-cultural relationships, to simply offer a way for people to meet. To achieve real success, providing good advice and useful knowledge are essential. From our work, we also often receive inquiries from men regarding Chinese ladies' intention and cultural issues. I understand completely their doubts and questions. Until now what information can be gleaned from the media about Chinese ladies today is still scarce, shallow and even biased. Moreover, although

Asian women in general have similar family values, Chinese ladies have their own particular views about love and marriage.

As the world enters the 21st century, everyone knows there is a big business opportunity in China. I would like to remind you there is also a big love opportunity in China. According to a CNNIC (China Internet Network Information Center) survey, in 2005 there were 110 million internet users in China. As this figure is rising quickly (no question about it), more and more Chinese will find love online because they find using the internet gives them much more choice indeed. Chinese are loving people and Chinese ladies are charming and intelligent. They are already proving to be a big, new, and exciting opportunity for love around the world!

If you are still searching for your love, if you are already dating a Chinese lady, or if you are interested in finding a Chinese heart but do not know how or want more confidence, please read this book. It uses many true stories to demonstrate to you the good ways to approach. It gives you insight on Chinese women and helps you to understand them comprehensively. It will open your eyes to a new world. It will bring you a true Chinese love and allow you to enjoy her charm and beauty happily forever.

There is a famous Chinese saying: "Know the other party as well as you know yourself, and you will win!"

Dawn Xiao Yan Li

February 2006
New Zealand

Chapter 1   *A Brief History of Chinese Marriage*

An understanding of Chinese history is obviously important for a good understanding of Chinese women. Just a reminder that here I am not lecturing you on Chinese history but rather telling you something to help you to get the most out of the following chapters, which will lead you most effectively to a Chinese heart.

1.   Men were dominant for thousands of years

China's varied and fascinating history dates back some 5000 years, during which it was ruled by a series of dynasties ranging from 2200 BC through the early part of the 20th century. A patriarchal society existed right from the beginnings of Chinese civilization. As the man was the one to bring food and money to the family, his important economic role ensured his place of leadership in marriage. This cultural structure has been the basis of male domination for millennia.

In traditional Chinese culture, men were likened to "sky" and women to "land". Marriage represented sky and land coming together, in which the sky covered the land and gave the land sunlight and water. Therefore the husband was a giver and the wife a receiver who had a duty to thank and obey her husband.

The husband had an absolute right to make decisions in the family and the wife was, in fact, just a tool to produce children and be a maid to the family. To maintain this system, over two thousand years ago the government enacted a law for men to be the rightful heir, in which all power and money was bequeathed from father to son. Men were not only rulers of the country, but also rulers of the family. This was the beginning of the longstanding Chinese tradition that "**men are superior and women are inferior; boys are precious and girls are cheap**". Even today, this tradition still applies in rural areas of China.

Here are some old Chinese traditions which are good examples of male power in marriage:

- Child Brides

A little girl given or sold to her future husband's house was called a child bride. This happened when the girl's family was too poor to raise her, or was desperate for money. The child bride could be as young as 12 or 13 years old: She was eligible as soon as she was able to do housework. It was a deal between the girl's parents and the boy's parents, made through a matchmaker. The girl may have never met her future husband.

The child bride was treated badly by her parents-in-law and "husband" at their home in most cases. Her status was actually that of a servant—to serve her parents-in-law and her "husband" rather than as daughter-in-law and "wife". Even later when she grew up and had her own children, she was still the servant for the extended family. There were many sad stories about child brides in old China. This tradition lasted until Mao established the People's Republic of China in 1949.

- Engagement and Wedding

The practice of the arranged marriage lasted for thousands of years in China. Either the parents or a matchmaker could arrange it. If a matchmaker was involved, all that was needed was approval from both sets of parents. The arrangement was based on a match of power, wealth and class between families, and had nothing to do with love. Again, the man and the woman may never have met before.

Once the arrangement was agreed, the man's family would take the initial action by sending engagement presents to the woman's family. This was a symbol that the man's family had purchased their daughter as a bride from the woman's family. If the engagement were later canceled for any reason, the engagement gifts (or their equivalent value) would be returned to the man's family.

On the wedding day, the family of the groom sent people to pick up the bride from her family home. It was an important day for both families because it declared to the public that the bride now belonged to her husband's family and was no longer a member of her own family. Even today, the wedding ceremony is much more meaningful to most Chinese than is the civil marriage registration.

Some of these customs regarding the engagement and wedding ceremony still remain today in China, although men and women are now each able to choose love on their own.

■   Parents-in-law

Once married, the lady was not only controlled by her husband, but also by her parents-in-law. Her own parents no longer had the right to influence, support or protect her. There was a famous Chinese saying: "a married daughter is spilled water", which meant you cannot have your daughter back after she is married. Parents-in-law had even more power over the wife's life than did her husband, because the husband had to listen to his parents as well. This double controlled system strengthened men's power even more in the marriage.

■   Concubines

Men could legally have concubines until the new China was established in 1949. A rich man could have one primary wife along with one or more secondary wives/concubines. The more concubines the man had, the richer or more powerful the man was presumed to be. To a rich or powerful man, women were not only his maids and baby producers, but also his playthings and decorations to show off. Therefore, the concubines he had were usually beautiful and much younger than he was.

The world moved forward, and in the early 20th century the Chinese concubine custom came to be challenged by the West. To maintain this privilege for Chinese men and protect their power in marriage, the world-renowned Chinese professor Mr. Gu was once asked by Westerners:

"Why can a man have many women while a woman can't have many men?"

Professor Gu replied:

"Having concubines is out of a husband's love and care to his wife. Man is as if a teapot and woman is as if a tea cup: A teapot with 4 tea cups can make a set, but a tea cup with 4 teapots cannot".

- Divorce, Remarriage and Sex

In the Chinese tradition, women could not choose divorce because men were in complete control. A husband could divorce his wife but his wife could not divorce him. If they didn't like her, then even the husband's parents had the right to fire their daughter-in-law without their son's approval.

Once divorced, men could marry again but women could not. In fact women could not remarry in any situation, including after being widowed. In the Song dynasty a thousand years ago, if a woman did not marry again after her husband died, she was highly rewarded by the government and respected by the public. In the later Yun dynasty, it even became law for a woman to remain an unmarried widow until her own death. Many widowed women couldn't face the hard life alone and chose suicide. To enforce its power on women at the time, the custom of binding feet was born.

If a woman had sex with a man prior to marriage, or had sex with someone who wasn't her husband, it could lead to her death (either suicide or at the hands of others) because she wouldn't have the face to live any more. If she lived, this black mark would stay with her for the rest of her life. Even today, for some Chinese men, to marry a virgin is still important.

The old traditions lasted for a long time in China. More recently, over the last few decades, China has made much progress. However since the traditions were deeply rooted, it has taken the Chinese people a lot of time and cost to move forward.

2.   Marriage reform over the last decades

The traditional Chinese marriage carried a social responsibility. It was important for power, wealth, politics, family reputation, public image and the like, but certainly not for love. Men were victims of society and women were victims of men. Thus the traditional Chinese marriage made victims of both men and women. The suffering finally reached its limit as people wanted to live for their own happiness. The long-lasting traditional marriage faced change at last.

> The traditional Chinese marriage carried a social responsibility. It was important for power, wealth, politics, family reputation, public image and the like, but certainly not for love.

2.1   1919 and the May Fourth Movement—Marriage Revolution

The May Fourth Movement is well known in Chinese history as the cultural movement that dared to confront the old systems and traditions. Begun on May 4, 1919 by young intellectuals at Beijing University, the May Fourth Movement also challenged the traditional Chinese marriage system. The movement was triggered by the tragic story of a certain Miss Zhao:

Miss Zhao's parents had arranged for her to marry a rich old man, Mr. Wu, to be his second wife after his first wife died. Miss Zhao had been to school and learned new thoughts. She didn't want to marry the old man, and spoke out to her parents to cancel the engagement. Her parents refused her and insisted she accept it. On the wedding day, Miss Zhao's parents forced her to go with the people from Mr. Wu's family who had come to pick her up. On her way to Mr. Wu's family, Miss Zhao killed herself with a razor blade.

As soon as Miss Zhao's tragedy was exposed, many people wrote newspaper articles criticizing the old arranged marriage. They said: "Miss Zhao was the victim of the traditional marriage and her death was caused by the evil social system". More and more intellectuals from different places in China joined the criticism, and a war of words soon erupted, attacking the old marriage system intensively. They cried out: "Love needs freedom! Marriage needs freedom! Happiness must be found by people themselves!"

The May Fourth Movement awakened the Chinese people from thousands of years of silence. But it was just the beginning of the long struggle against the traditional ideas of marriage, and of the equally long search for true love, freedom in life, and equal rights for men and women. The battle between the old and new, with its advances and retreats, inevitably caused pain to those caught up in it, and many fell victim to the war. However no one could stop it and history had to move forward.

2.2 Mao's time—Political love and marriage

When Chairman Mao founded the People's Republic of China in 1949, the new marriage law was born. For the first time in China, freedom of marriage and equal rights for men and women were written into law. The new China brought women the right to choose love and marriage for themselves. This was a landmark in the history of marriage in China. Unfortunately these "equal rights and freedoms" soon had a political flavor.

Immediately on coming to power, Mao launched political movements one after another. These movements, and the resulting importance of each person's political identity, began to take control of Chinese personal life. People were classified according to their political status: Red class—from worker, peasant or military families; White class—from intellectual families; and Black class—from rich or other politically blacklisted families. The Red class was superior and the other two classes were bad.

To be able to have "a good and promising life", marrying someone from the Red class was critical. Because of this, political status became the first priority for people to consider in marriage. Under the intense official and social pressure, love disappeared once again. Countless people had to give up their true love and marry someone from the Red class so they could find a good job, get promoted at work, win respect from others, and have a good future for their children. In the meantime, the people from the White and Black classes couldn't find anyone to marry—and in the end this became quite a social problem.

> The Cultural Revolution of the 1960s brought China to a time in which emotions were heavily restrained. Intimacy disappeared both in public and at home, and even heterosexual intimacy was held to be criminal.

As the political movements heated up, only one person in the entire country was accepted as worthy of anyone's love-Chairman Mao. The Cultural Revolution of the 1960s brought China to a time in which emotions were heavily restrained. Intimacy disappeared both in public and at home, and even heterosexual intimacy was held to be criminal. There was no place for people to date because all the parks were either closed or guarded by civil authorities. If a couple were found to be dating in public, they were abused and/or beaten.

During this period, men and women dressed the same in green or blue, and no scenes of romance were allowed in movies, plays or books. In fact all forms of entertainment were used for political promotion. No one dared to show his or her personal emotions and desires in public— this would have led to severe punishment for having put oneself above Chairmen Mao.

In addition, it was common for husbands and wives to live separately in different parts of China, either because they were forced to or because of their own motivation in respect of the needs of the revolution. Divorce was very rare because every comrade was supposed to put his or her attention solely on the revolutionary task at hand. Mao and his political movements were the center of people's lives for almost thirty years.

2.3   Marriage today—Confusion

Mao died in 1976, and in the eighties the intensive focus on Mao started to wane. Although now liberated from political movements and restraints on emotion, the abrupt immersion of the Chinese people into the sea of the global economy created new challenges for love and marriage.

Adding to the difficulties of adapting to new concepts, the Chinese mind is still, at its most basic level, deeply rooted in traditional thought. The formal education regarding marriage was written 2,200 years ago in the "Li Ji", a central text of Confucianism. This classic work formalized the rules for people to follow in all respects, including politics, philosophy, daily life, the morality of both men and women, and the roles of husband and wife. More recently Mao's sayings in the form of his "Little Red Book" were the only allowed form of education. Although the old thoughts have been reformed over the last few decades, people haven't yet had a chance to absorb new ways of thinking.

Currently Chinese people are facing many conflicts, e.g. family values versus career success, freedom of marriage versus social acceptance, true love versus material attraction, modern choice versus Chinese tradition. On one side are an increasing divorce rate, covert concubines, and extramarital affairs, and on the other a longing for true love and a lasting quality marriage…Chinese people are lost and confused.

Moreover, as China opens its door to the West and the Internet continues to become more and more widely available, the Western influence is gradually reaching beyond the impersonal realm of economics and official actions. Correctly understanding Western thoughts on relationships and marriage, and taking proper advantage of those ideas, has become another challenge for the Chinese.

The new era has brought tremendous change and a lot for Chinese to learn. Unfortunately, compared to Westerners, Chinese have been told little of love and marriage. Even today, being rich or powerful is still the symbol of a person's success in China. The media often glorifies people who are successful in business or politics. There are tons of books and courses to teach people how to make money, how to get promoted in careers, how to find a well-paid job and how to send children to famous schools, but very few books to teach people about relationships and marriage. Of the books available on the market, 99% are simply translations of foreign books and are neither adjusted for, nor understood by, the Chinese people.

> Traditional family values still play an important role for Chinese, and particularly for Chinese women. They want to have a good marriage and family, and they want to be taught how to achieve these goals.

In general, there has been no education on love and marriage since "Li Ji". Ironically, it is considered shameful to talk about love in public, even though love is a basic need for people in life, just like water and food. Even if a person has both money and power, he or she is not happy without love. As well, traditional family values still play an important role for Chinese, and particularly for Chinese women. They want to have a good marriage and family, and they want to be taught how to achieve these goals.

Evolution is driven by people's needs, and any evolutionary cycle is born with a process of confusion, pain and learning. There is no doubt that China will have another landmark in its marriage history soon. With the support of the world, China will finally reach for the real meanings of "true love" and "equal rights"!

Chapter 2   Chinese Women in Dating and Marriage

A Gentleman from Asian Promise once said:

"In the depths of my heart and soul I feel that all humans on planet earth are the outer manifestation and living essence of the same spirit. It is our cultural influences and indoctrinations that tend to make individuals appear to behave somewhat differently. And even though we as people of the world have different outward appearances, we all have the same inner spirit, the 'human spirit'...."

1.   The past: Victims of marriage

There was no term for dating in Chinese tradition. Marriage was arranged either when both parties were still children or as soon as they grew up. Women had neither the right nor the chance to choose their own life partner until the May Fourth Movement.

As explained in Chapter 1, men were victims of society and women were victims of men. Marriage was the best example of this. In order to maintain the power and wealth in the family and pass them to the next male generation, the wife became a necessary tool to produce offspring and to be a maid to look after her husband and son. Men held absolute financial rights in the family and left no ground for women to stand up for themselves. The ancient book called the "Liji" [1] had set up the following rules for married women to obey:

- Subordinate status: A married woman was subordinate to her husband. If her husband died, she was supposed to be subordinate to her son.

- Morals: These were judged by personality, appearance, speech and ability. Generally speaking, a wife was to be tender, virtuous, clean, neat, quiet, polite and able to do housework. Standing out through exceptional intellect or appearance was not encouraged.

- After her husband died, she wasn't supposed to marry again.

- The husband or his family had the right to divorce the wife if her parents in law didn't like her, or if she didn't give a birth to a boy, had an extramarital affair, had uncured diseases, was jealous of her husband's concubines, etc.

- She couldn't leave her husband for any reason. "Marry chicken and live with chicken, marry dog and live with dog" was the Chinese woman's fate in marriage.

Men were superior and women were inferior, a situation which lasted for thousands of years of Chinese history. Marriage had the effect of further debasing a woman's life and trammeling her freedom.

2.   Chinese women today

The situation started to change beginning with the May Fourth Movement of 1919. Following the hard struggles over the last few decades, the social and marriage position of Chinese women is today much improved. Equal rights are granted in both their professional and personal lives. However because of the old traditions and the reality of differences between men and women, Chinese women today face the new task of finding their place in life and living it in a balanced way.

2.1   Chinese women in dating

Generally speaking, "dating" did not begin until after the May Fourth Movement. Nowadays most dating is based on love. However, because the purpose of dating is for marriage, which still applies for most Chinese women today, the dating has to be the "right dating". "Right dating" includes social acceptance and the wishes of the parents, demonstrating that the traditional values still have influence.

Today many Chinese women have a good education, particularly those from urban areas. They understand that they should choose their own lives and not let others control them, and that personality is more important than social and material concerns. This is easy to say but not so easy to do in real life. True love can be crushed under social and parental pressure.

Although such pressure may affect Chinese women in how they choose a date, it cannot stop them from finding love. When love cannot be found with the "right dating", Chinese women will stand up bravely to challenge the old tradition.

Lan was one of our Asian Promise members from a remote city in China. She was a senior editor in a newspaper and was highly respected by her fellows. She and her ex-husband divorced when her son was only 4 years old. Her ex-husband was alcoholic and was violent when he drank. When Lan left him, her father and brother forced her to go back to him. Later they stopped her from marrying her new lover.

Time flew, and Lan was soon 50 years old with an 18 year old son. Realizing her son would soon be leaving, she decided to find someone to love and keep her company. But this was almost a dream in China. Chinese men didn't like older divorced women. With the support of her son and of Asian Promise, Lan began her international search for love on the Internet. She didn't tell her family and kept it quiet at work. She knew her choice could cause her to lose both family and job.

"There's a will, there's a way". Lan found her Internet love one year later. The second time her boyfriend flew from America to see her, Lan decided to tell her father she was going to get engaged. It was a hard decision. As she expected, the news provoked her father and brother again. They swore at her and criticized her, saying her finding another man at her age would cause them to lose face. They laughed at her finding a foreign man, and threatened her with expulsion from the family if she were to actually marry him.

Love is powerful and China is now different from the past after all. In the end, Lan married her American heart and is now living happily with her husband in the USA.

Even though Lan's experience was not common in today's China, it showed that tradition could not stand up to her determined efforts. One's own attitude is the most important thing in China today. Most times the influence of old tradition is not from the outside, but from the inside of the person. The people themselves are still confined by old Chinese thought. Here is a typical example from my work:

I often receive letters from our ladies telling me how young and beautiful they are. They believe they have the advantage in finding superior (rich and powerful) men to marry, because of their beauty and youth. As this is still true in China, ladies think it applies in the West as well.

Once upon a time, a beautiful young member of ours, who was sincerely looking for someone to marry, received a very nice letter from an Englishman. In order to impress him, she replied with lots of photos of her in bikini outfits. This Englishman was puzzled and thought she was looking for a sex partner.

A Chinese woman's attitude towards love depends on her education level, social class, living standard, life experience, family influence, and so on, which can all differ widely from person to person. While many ladies put love first, there are some who still primarily value appearance and material wealth; while many strive for true love, some still emphasize social acceptance; many choose their own dates but others like their dates to be chosen for them. Other examples: making the initial move or enjoying being chased, acceptance of splitting the bill on a date versus expecting men to pay the bill, accepting sex before marriage or believing in the importance of virginity prior to marriage.

> One's own attitude is the most important thing in China today. Most times the influence of old tradition is not from the outside, but from the inside of the person.

Having experienced all of the above at Asian Promise, we see that Chinese women are on their way to change. Against deep-rooted ancient tradition, Chinese women are open and willing to learn new things. They are also intelligent and devoted. They can see the modern approach is the ultimate way to have a true love and good marriage. Therefore, like Lan, they are willing to make all the necessary efforts to achieve their goals.

2.2   Chinese women in marriage

As result of Mao's time, Chinese ladies today have equal rights with men. This is quite similar to women in other advanced countries, e.g. they prefer to share the housework with their husbands and to continue to work after marriage.

However the traditional form of marriage and family still has its impact. The family in which the man is stronger and has a more respected or more financially rewarding job is still much admired. There are still many women who intend to improve their quality of life through marriage, particularly those from the more impoverished places in China. That said, most Chinese women want their marriage to be love-based. Marriages for power and money only are not popular today, and are criticized and looked down on by the Chinese people.

The mixture of the old and new ways of thinking has resulted in Chinese women being able to have a flexible role in marriage today:

1.   "Virtuous wife and good mother" and "career success"

Chinese women have struggled between "virtuous wife and good mother" and "career success" since Mao's time. Indeed, women and men can never be the same. During the Mao period, Chinese women had difficulty playing their multiple roles in life. In order to work the same as a man, for example, a woman had only 56 days leave from work before and after her baby was born. Between work and home, they were running like rabbits.

When I was few months old, my mother had to dash back home by bicycle to breast feed me at her lunchtime break every day. It took her 15 minutes to go home and another 15 minutes to come back to work. This left her no time to actually eat lunch. My mother worked in a children's hospital and looked after dozens of other people's children, but left me to be looked after by a distant family relative from the countryside.

The situation has changed since the 80's, after Mao's death. Nowadays women have a choice. Many Chinese women want to have a happy marriage and family, as well as a successful career. When personal life and career are in conflict, some of them tend to be held back by inertia left over from Mao's power, even though they long for a contented life with their spouse and children. They appear career-minded, but it is a different model than the Western idea. There are, of course, some Chinese women who are career-minded in the Western sense, but not many.

Chinese women are now learning to keep the balance between being a good wife and mother and achieving career success. They are beginning to understand that if you want everything, you may achieve nothing. They are learning that sometimes you have to choose.

Recently I received a letter from my 24 year old niece in Beijing. She told me she was going to get married next month, and would resign from her job soon afterwards. She was very happy and couldn't wait to have children. Her fiancé had a well-paid job and his income would be enough for the two of them and their children. I know my niece is typical of the more traditional girls, and will thoroughly enjoy her life as a wife and mother.

My niece is a lucky one because she knew what she wanted and was able to achieve it. There are still many Chinese women who must continue to work to support the family, even though they would prefer to stay at home.

2.   Dependence and independence

The Chinese woman wants to find a good, strong husband on whom to depend, but she also wants freedom and independence.

Divorced for three years, one of my best friends in China recently met a Chinese Canadian man. He asked her to move to Canada after marriage. She couldn't make up her mind because she didn't want to leave her job. On one hand she wanted to find someone on whom she could depend, but on the other hand she worried she would lose her freedom in the marriage. She believed financial independence is critical in marriage. Going to a new place meant she wouldn't be able to find a job straight away, and she would be completely dependent on her husband.

I have found from my work at Asian Promise that many Chinese ladies have worries similar to those of my girlfriend. On the surface, you may think she works for money; in fact, she works for freedom. Mao's education of "financial status determines one's social status" still applies to Chinese. Because of this, Chinese women are likely to attribute their past bad times to a lack of financial independence. Social welfare systems and organizations which support women, while more common in Western countries, are still underdeveloped in China and are not familiar to Chinese women.

3. Immediate family and extended family

Nowadays if there is a choice, many Chinese couples choose to live on their own. In other cases they may not have their own house, or they may need help from their parents or *vice versa*. Although parents-in-law have lost their power in modern days, parents still play a more important role in the marriage than is common in the West.

Mao's institution of equal rights gave married couples equal responsibility for both sets of parents. The one child policy of the 80's has resulted in most couples today being responsible for four old people. Although rest homes are now available in China, old people are reluctant to go and young people feel guilty sending them. Adult children still have heavy responsibilities in looking after their aged parents.

Moreover, in order to have a good marriage, it is still important for Chinese women to please their parents-in-law. The old traditions and new responsibilities allow Chinese women to play many roles in their own and in their extended families.

4.   Choice of divorce and family values

Today Chinese women have the same right to initiate a divorce as men, but they are not so willing to use it. More than Western women, Chinese women find marriage and family so important they make every effort to keep it intact.

The ancient traditions also make it difficult to choose divorce. Chinese men do not favor women who have had a divorce or who already have children. This makes it very difficult for these Chinese women to find a new love and marriage, and to preserve a father's love for their children. As well, sometimes the financial situation makes it difficult for them to choose divorce. These considerations have made Chinese women more tolerant, patient and willing to expend extra effort when their marriage is in difficulty.

In summary, although China has entered modern times, most Chinese women still have strong family values. Marriage is very important in their life. In the marriage, the husband is in charge of outside duties and the wife is in charge of inside (home) duties; the husband takes the lead and the wife follows, the husband makes more money with a better career and the wife spends more time at home with the children. This is still the mainstream thought, even today. The difference from the past is that most marriages today are based on love and respect for each other. Chinese women are not just baby producers and maids anymore.

> Although China has entered modern times, most Chinese women still have strong family values. Marriage is very important in their life.

3. How Chinese women differ from other Asian women

Although all Asian women have similar marriage and family values, Chinese women have their own views stemming from the particular historical background previously discussed. Chinese women also have an appearance different from other Asian women. Compared with other Asian women, Chinese women are taller with fine and fair skin physically, and more reserved emotionally.

Unlike some Asian countries that had been Western colonies for a long time, China is very self-contained and closed. Therefore Chinese women are not familiar with Western culture and customs, and are unable to take to the Western culture as quickly as those Asian women who are from Western colonial countries. Their spoken English is also not as good. However their ability to read and write English may surprise you, even if they speak very little. The reason for this is simple: they don't have much chance to practice in China!

> Chinese women are more open-minded and westernized as a result of Mao's influence, but still have characteristics held over from older ideas of family values.

Chinese women have received benefits from the Mao era. They are open-minded, curious and well educated in general. They are willing to learn new things. They are not as submissive or religious as are many Buddhist East Asians and Catholic Filipinas, and not so bonded with their cultural traditions as are some other Asian women. Mao's elimination of ALL culture left Chinese women a blank slate and thus more open-minded in many ways. Chinese women also believe in equal rights for men and women. They expect and appreciate husbands doing housework, they are willing to help the family financially, and they want to be their husband's soul mate—all of which are very similar to what Western women want in marriage today.

A simple way to describe the difference between Chinese women and other Asian women is: Chinese women are more open-minded and westernized as a result of Mao's influence, but still have characteristics held over from older ideas of family values.

4. How Chinese women differ from Western women

In late 2004 I conducted an email survey for the chapter on Western attitudes toward love and marriage in my book (in Chinese) [2]. I sent a questionnaire to fifty Western men from Asian Promise, ranging from thirty to sixty years of age. One of the twelve questions I posed was:

"Do you think Chinese ladies are different from Western ladies? If yes, how?"

The answers I received were all definitely "yes", noting both cultural and physical differences. The results were very close to those found in my own cross-cultural experience. The answers are summarized below [3]:

- *Western women tend to be the equal of their male counterparts. Because of this many tend to act like men. Chinese women are not afraid to be women. Chinese women have opinions and work hard and disagree with their loved ones too, but they still remain feminine.*

- *Western women are more direct, outgoing and experienced in love. They know what they want and achieve it with much confidence. Chinese women are more timid, more reserved, and less confident. They often put others' views and feelings before their own, which causes them to lose some of their own personality.*

- *Western women put more value on the quality of the marriage, while Chinese women give more value to the marriage itself. Therefore Chinese women are more willing to overcome their difficulties or even live with the difficulties within the marriage, rather than abandoning it entirely.*

- *Western woman are more independent than Chinese women in general.*

- *Chinese women are willing to work hard and save money because the memory of their old lives is still fresh. They tend to worry about tomorrow rather than to enjoy today.*

- *They have a different style of beauty: Chinese women have black hair, brown eyes, smooth hairless skin, more petite bodies, and exhibit a quiet oriental elegance.*

5.   Why choose Chinese ladies?

There are many reasons for Western men to choose Chinese ladies. It really depends on the person and varies from one man to the next. Doing the research for my book, I also asked: "*Why do you choose a Chinese lady for your wife?*" Below I have selected some of the replies. I hope these will give you an answer from a personal perspective:

Scott, 40 years old from America:

I am attracted to the physical appearance of Chinese women. I like the sound of the Chinese accent when they speak English, as well as the sound of the Mandarin Chinese language. I also like the attitude of many Chinese women nowadays—very curious about the West, and excited about the internationalization currently happening in China. I am also extremely impressed with the highly educated Chinese women I have met.

In addition, I have heard that some Chinese women think Western men treat them better than they would be treated in a traditional Chinese marriage—this makes me feel like I have something which will be pleasing to a Chinese wife.

Richard, 36 years old from England/New Zealand:

As an Englishman I had very little contact with Asian women or their cultures before I moved to Hong Kong. In fact I was pretty ignorant about Asia in general. I arrived in Hong Kong in 1997 to experience the handover to China and ended up staying. After a while I became more adjusted to the Chinese look. I now found I was looking at beauty quite unparalleled in the typical Caucasian. Chinese women's bodies are slim, their skin is silky smooth, often hairless, and their bodies have beautiful curves. I also discovered that looks and characteristics varied dramatically across China.

I met my Chinese wife and was immediately bowled over by her. Not only was she very good looking but also she had such an attractive personality. Like many single women on the Asian Promise website, she was degree qualified, had been married before and had a child. For me, the child was an added bonus, and for her she was just interested to find a man who would look after her and her child and respect her for her personality and not only her looks. She found these qualities existed in men with a Western outlook but were rare in men she had met in China, who, in her experience, tend not to be interested in ladies who have been married before, and who place a huge importance on looks.

Now let me tell you why to choose Chinese ladies from my personal experience:

- *They will love and support you with all their heart*
- *They are well educated*
- *They have an open mind*
- *They are charming and elegant*
- *They are curious to learn new things*
- *They are enchanted by the West*
- *Their language is like poetry*
- *Their skin is silky smooth*
- *They always look younger than you thought*
- *Your children will be beautiful and…*
- *They want you!*

David, 45 years old from America:

I didn't start my search to find a Chinese lady. I have lived in other parts of Asia and have always enjoyed the beauty of the women. I searched online and found a woman who just happened to be Chinese. I think Chinese ladies have an exotic beauty that makes my heart jump. I think there are many differences between Chinese and American women. Culture, attitudes about family, how to raise children are just some of the many differences. I like the differences. My future wife and I will work hard to overcome all the obstacles.

K.C., 60 years old from America:

Because of my age, I am limited in who would accept me in my country. American women put a premium on youth and are unforgiving in their acceptance of older men as potential mates. I understand the rationale behind their reasoning, and have no problems dealing with this attitude. On the contrary, I do believe that a Chinese lady would appreciate such virtues as knowledge and wisdom, which often come with a man of my age.

Jay, 40 years old from America:

I chose a Chinese woman because I have had an attraction to Asian women and Asian culture for many years and especially Chinese. Some are attracted to blondes. I find Asian women to be the most beautiful. I like the Chinese theory about "Yin" and "Yang". They are not different, but not alike. They do not detract from the other and they complement each other and fit together perfectly. My wife makes me a more complete person as I do for her. We become one in spirit, mind and body.

I am sure that there are women in my country who are sweet and smart as my Chinese girlfriend, but I was not able to find them. That is why I am so grateful for your Asian Promise service!

Paduos, 27 years old from Italy:

Well I never had experience with a Chinese woman, but I feel they are sweet and different from Western women. I believe they look after their husbands and care about family.

Darrell, 36 years old from America:

My first marriage failed. I learned a lesson and decided to develop a new relationship slowly. This is why I chose a long distance relationship. I searched online and found my Chinese wife on Asian Promise. It took us two years to get married.

Many people are surprised by the fact I found someone outside the USA and wonder how I can maintain a relationship with someone so far away. They also don't realize she is as close as my heart and only a computer screen away. We spend three to six hours a day Seeing, Chatting, and Talking—that is more than many couples do when they live together. There are a great number of things I would like to say but don't know how. I just know I am the happiest I have been in many years. I wrote something for her awhile back and placed it on my site, it is an analogy of Love:

LOVE is like a seed, not a seed of a flower, But the seed of a Redwood Tree that lives for centuries, Once the seed is planted it needs to be nurtured so it can get a healthy start in life, If it is not given a healthy start it will wither and die or be stunted and never reach its fullest potential, However if given a good start it will take hold with deep roots and grow stronger each day, During its lifetime it will suffer many hardships as shown by its scars and if it is not too severe it will come back and continue growing until the day it dies, But even then it stands as a monument to what it was, In time it will fade and decay, But even then it will give of itself to help its offspring get their healthy start in life.

6. Why do Chinese ladies choose you?

As Western men have many reasons to choose Chinese ladies, so do Chinese ladies have many reasons to choose you. For them, too, it also depends on the person and differs from one to another. The following are reasons I have seen in my experience with Asian Promise:

■ More choice

Many people cannot find their match nearby. In order to have more choice, they must broaden their search. As China opens its door and the Internet becomes more widely available, international dating becomes possible. As the world become more and more international, the dating market will become bigger and bigger. More choice means more chance for her to find the best match.

Moreover, Chinese men do not prefer women who have had a divorce or who already have children, which makes it very difficult for these Chinese women to find a new marriage inside China. Because of this, these Chinese women choose to search for love outside of China (an important reason that Asian Promise has experienced). These women do not mind leaving their own country, giving up their well-paid jobs or meeting the challenges of a new culture—they want love and to be loved again.

- Improving quality of life

Improving one's quality of life through marriage is a tradition in China. Although nowadays many single Chinese women have a good income and life, there are still many women from remote places in China living a more basic way of life. To them, the Western world is a modern world and offers a better life and better opportunities. A good quality of life is a good foundation of the marriage. These women want to find a husband to love and to be loved, and they also hope he will bring them a better life. Sometimes a better life doesn't mean money and a house, but rather spiritual nourishment.

- Love of Western culture

Many educated Chinese women have been to the West or have had experience with Westerners in China. They are familiar with Western culture and like the culture very much. They like Western gentlemen who respect ladies and treat them well in public and at home, qualities which are not commonly seen in Chinese men within China. Being a "Big man" both in public and at home are still common in China.

> Chinese women like the ability of Western men to put personality above age and appearance, and Westerners accept, and enjoy, a Chinese woman's children as well as the woman herself.

They like the ability of Western men to put personality above age and appearance, as well as their more refined tastes in sex, which is not solely based on physical needs. Westerners accept, and enjoy, a Chinese woman's children as well as the woman herself. All in all, Chinese women are pleased with the Western attitude towards love and marriage.

■ Physical attraction

To some Chinese women, Western men look sexier and more attractive—they are muscular, large, have clear facial features, hairy skin, blue eyes, and are gentle and humorous.

■ Chance

Falling in love without expecting to: In this case, the couples are normally not aware of the difference in race or culture before falling in love. In the end, it is two people together. Cultures, beliefs and values are all worked out by the people. As the world becomes more internationally connected, more and more cross-cultural love, relationships and marriages will fill this category.

■ Money or passport

Just like some women anywhere else in the world, there are some Chinese women who want money or a foreign passport and will use Western men to get them. These women are different from women who want to improve their quality of life through love and marriage. They are not interested in love, but in material gain. Amongst these women, some are not aware of the existence of things more valuable than money. Their attitude towards life might change if they could receive a better education.

I understand that women wanting money and a passport are big concerns for Western men when they date ladies from poorer countries. I will address this issue again in the following chapters.

> **A Gentleman from Asian Promise once said:**
> (continued from his saying at the beginning of this chapter)
>
> *"…We as humanity must learn to love each other and live together in peace. Intercultural love and marriages are one way to bridge the gulf of misunderstandings and intolerance, cultivates cultural awareness and diversity, and lead to a better world in which to live."*

Reference

[1] A basic text of Confucianism, written 2,200 years ago, that formalized the rules for people to follow in all aspects of life, including politics, philosophy, daily life, men and women's morality, roles of husband and wife, etc…

[2] Connecting You to Love/Finding True Love Online, written by Li Xiao Yan and published by Cosmos Books (Hong Kong)/China Youth Press (Mainland China).

[3] This information is not a formal study of a large group and is presented here for your reference only.

Chapter 3   Dating Chinese Women

> **What is the most important key in finding a life partner?**
>
> "Sincerity *is the most important key in finding true love and a life partner. Good communication, respect, confidence, patience... follow.*"
>
> Answer from the 2003 Asian Promise survey [1]

1.   Your honesty wins her honesty

"Honest" is the most used word in the thousands of personal profiles that we have received at Asian Promise. Commonly seen are the phrases "being honest" or "looking for an honest one". Honesty is the first quality that 99% of people are looking for in a marriage relationship. This is not just the case for women, but for men as well. The best way to be treated as you would like is to treat others the same way. Your honesty will win her honesty.

Chinese women appreciate the openness of Western men very much. The Western man will generally make his intentions known to the lady, which is whether he wants a long term relationship, a short tem relationship or just a one night stand. Chinese men are typically different. Sometimes the Chinese man doesn't tell the woman his real intentions because he wants to date her but doesn't want to marry her. If he tells her the truth, he would lose his chance to date the woman because for many Chinese ladies, marriage is still the only reason for dating. Because of cultural differences, Chinese women are more cautious about the man's dating intentions and more hesitant to ask than are Western women. So they are very grateful for Western openness.

Chinese women understand that Western people may have different reasons for dating (I explained this to them in my book [2]), and they respect your modern choice as long as you are honest with them. As a marriage relationship only website, Asian Promise has offered an excellent and ideal service to Chinese ladies. Chinese women like us and trust us because we guarantee our ladies that 95% of our men are looking for a marriage relationship [1].

However people are not always on the level. It is impossible to completely avoid those who misrepresent themselves. We have experienced two types of people who don't tell the whole truth. One is not looking for a serious relationship at all and is just playing games, and the other is looking for a serious relationship, but using dishonest ways. Here are some examples of the first kind:

We received letters from two different lady members within a three month period. They both told us they had just fallen in love with their boyfriend when he suddenly died in a car accident. One of the ladies was so sad she couldn't carry on her normal life. Because the whole thing sounded odd, we investigated and found their boyfriends were actually the same man, who had sent them the same handsome photos and sweet letters. In order to prevent more ladies being cheated by him, we told all our lady members his trick. It was both surprising and ridiculous to find out that the "dead" man was still dating two additional ladies from our website. Apparently this "dead" man is still alive and actively dating on other sites.

Another man, who seemed to be more real than the "dead" one, dated one lady a few years ago. They met through a friend. According to her, he was a very generous, polite and loving gentleman. He met her in China and traveled there from America to see her three more times within the next 6 months. However he never mentioned his intentions with her during his visits. When she asked him, he said it was too soon to talk. She had helped him to print his book and buy building materials in China. Finally it turned out that he had no intention at all of building a relationship and was simply using her to do business in China.

Those who play games do not have a heart. They are not in my interest to discuss here. What I would like to pay attention to is the second kind who are seriously looking for a life partner, but using dishonest methods:

One of our ladies worried that she couldn't find anyone to love her because of her age, so she made her age five years younger in her profile. With the day of her boyfriend's first visit fast approaching, she became so nervous that she urgently asked us for help—but it was already too late.

Another lady had met several men through us over one year period, but none of the men was interested in continuing with her after they met in person. She asked me why and I couldn't give her a good answer until I met her in person too. She looked too different from her photo.

Some of our men chatted with several different ladies from our website at the same time, but told each lady he was only chatting with her. This continued until one day the lady received his emails addressed to someone else.

Some men didn't tell ladies they were only separated but not divorced. Some men didn't tell ladies they were alcoholics or used drugs.

Although you may think you have a good reason for being dishonest because you are looking for true love, your prospective partner may still choose to leave you. Being honest is so important in the marriage relationship that he or she may leave you not because of your age, your looks, your contacts with other potential partners or your marital status, but because of your dishonesty. I have said to ladies:

"You could explain to him later that you have made your age younger because you want to win his heart, but in the meantime you have also lost his faith in you. In the end, he is not disappointed by your real age or appearance;

he is disappointed by your dishonesty. If you want to win him and you want to have an honest relationship, being honest yourself is the first action to take."

And the same goes for you: Tell her the truth. If she can see your honesty and your intentions, she wouldn't mind to take a risk. Love is a risk, like anything else. Being honest is the best way to reduce the love risk and a most wise way to achieve real happiness.

There are other ways to prevent cheaters, such as using background checks, meeting through friends, and charging member fees, however one's own common sense and wisdom are the keys. Being honest and wise will help you and her to make a good choice. Those who play games will lose them in the face of honesty and wisdom, because people know that a real relationship needs a real you!

> If she can see your honesty and your intentions, she wouldn't mind to take a risk. Love is a risk, like anything else. Being honest is the best way to reduce the love risk and a most wise way to achieve real happiness.

2.   Dating her online

As the Internet enters our lives, more and more people have chosen it as a way to search for love. It is a great way to search internationally. The increasing number of cross-cultural relationships and marriages today owes a great deal to Internet dating. Since it is such an important way for people to meet today, it is necessary for us to have a look at dating Chinese women online.

Benefits of Online Dating

1. More choice—increases the chance to find a life partner

2. Easy access—just needs a computer and an Internet connection

3. Good independence and efficiency

4. Flexibility—anytime, anywhere, casual dress, shaving optional, etc.

5. Fast communication in many ways—email, online chatting, voice, photo…

6. Focus on one's inner quality rather than outer appearance

7. Promotes the importance of good communication

8. Easily overcome the fear of rejection

9. Inexpensive—free or paid membership (much less than traditional methods)

10. Good safety—don't need to meet until you know each other

2.1 Choosing the right site

There are thousands of dating websites on the Internet nowadays. Surfing among them, you feel lost at sea, not knowing in which direction lies your home port. However if you know what you want you will quickly find your way, and everything soon becomes easy and clear. For example, if you want a marriage, you have ruled out at least 70% of the dating choices. If you want an Asian bride and particularly a Chinese bride as a life-partner, your choice is further narrowed. Finally you will find you have moved from sea to river, or even to a small stream. Following the stream you will find exactly where you want to be.

Many people dream of falling in love in a natural and romantic way. Unfortunately this is not a wise thing to do for online dating. Meeting people on the Internet is different from meeting them in real life. It is easy to create a false impression. At best you waste your time, and at worst you could end up with a disaster. The best way to avoid this unhappiness is to make it clear what you want right from the start, and more so when you are searching for a life partner on a multi-purpose dating site or a more entertainment-oriented site. The way you meet someone is not the only chance you will have to feel romantic. Romance can happen in lovers at any time. In fact, each of the lovers from our site has had their own unique romance, all of which are rather touching.

To save time and risk, I suggest you choose dating sites that are for marriage only. It's even better if the site charges money to all members, which tends to ensure they are much more seriously looking for marriage, and that the profiles are much more real and valid. Most dating sites offer free membership to women but charge fees for men. From my experience, it is also important to ask the ladies to pay. Success requires commitment by both parties. Paying a membership fee not only shows you are serious, but also makes you more committed and determined, which are very important factors in finding a life long partner.

Many of our lady members have had experience with free dating websites (e.g. Asian Friend Finder) either directly or indirectly (through dating agencies who register them in those free dating websites). They tell us they often receive emails from men asking for sex only. Before they sign up with us, they ask me if Western men are only looking for sex and if the success stories on our Asian Promise site are true. I have to explain that the reason they have this impression and doubt is because they have been looking for love in all the wrong places, and finding the wrong things.

I feel it is a shame that many Chinese women have a skewed image of Western men. I often explain to ladies that Western men can have more than one reason for dating (not solely dating leading to marriage), and I advise them to respect these choices. I suggest ladies choose the correct dating sites (those focused on marriage) or make it clear to the man that they are only looking for a marriage relationship. Because of this, I also suggest you do the same thing. You deserve to be treated seriously because you are looking for a serious relationship!

When you choose dating sites, I also suggest you be aware of dishonest ones. We have had some nasty experiences with fraudulent sites:

Several times we found and were told by others that our ladies' profiles appeared on other dating sites. Those sites copied our ladies' profiles onto their websites in order to attract men to become their paid members. They were not only infringing our copyright and offending our ladies, but also defrauding unsuspecting men. In reality, they don't have the contact details for the ladies, and some of profiles have been out of date for a long time.

For all of the reasons above, I sincerely suggest to all gentlemen who are looking for a serious relationship not to start your love search until you have done a good deal of research browsing the dating sites. A good start is the beginning of your success. Your seriousness in this respect will bring you serious success.

Tips on Judging Dating Sites

1. Paid or unpaid membership?
2. Long distance dating or local dating?
3. Your emails replied to personally or automatically?
4. Contact phone number for website available?
5. Member profiles updated frequently or infrequently?
6. Members directly from the site or through other agencies?
7. Site contents dynamic, consistent…or not?
8. Site offers good support information in addition to profiles?

2.2 Your profile

Your profile is your first impression to her. Whether you can catch her eye or not will depend completely on your profile. From my experience, although the profile text and the photos are both important, men pay more attention to the woman's photos while women pay as much attention to what he writes as to the men's photos. So spending more time to write a good profile is your first step to get her attention. The following are my suggestions to help you to write a good profile:

1. Be sincere, direct and simple

    Since sincerity is the most important factor in finding true love and a life partner, letting her see that you are sincerely looking for a life partner is very important. Remember that English is not her first language, and try to keep your writing simple, easy to understand, straightforward, not too romantic and not too philosophical. To make it sincere and simple, I suggest you write your profile in around 150 words (certainly not less than 50, nor more than 200).

2. Tell her something about yourself

    Tell her something about your interests, your work/career, your family, your lifestyle and your goals and values. By reading these, she can have a general picture of you and your personality, so she can see whether or not she is interested in you. Don't go into too much detail. It's better to leave room to expand on things later in your future communication with her.

    If you are interested in Chinese or Asian culture, please say so. If you are in good health or have a good financial status, say this as well.

3. Show your respect to her

    When you state the qualities of the person for whom you are looking, please don't let her feel you are bossy or "Big" e.g. *"you should look after me"*, *"you should obey me"*, *"you must cook"*, *"you are submissive"*…

    As I said in my previous chapter:

    "Chinese women advocate equal rights for women and men. For example: they expect and appreciate husbands doing housework,

they are willing to help the family financially, they want to be their husband's soul mate...all these are very similar to what Western women want in marriage today."

Your respect is very important to her. Otherwise you will turn her off without any doubt indeed. Moreover, don't set too many criteria for your date. As we all know, no one is perfect.

4. Don't be sex-centric

    Although sex is important in a marriage relationship, don't make it the core of your profile. To women, sex comes after love. If you make sex a big thing in your profile, she will think that you are looking for sex and not love.

5. Don't use symbols

    Too many symbols (e.g. ^_^) creates an impression of being a game player, and of being lazy and childish. It is a shallow way to show your humor. It is okay to use them in your communication later when you know each other more, but not in your profile.

6. Use her country's system of measurement

    Many men use feet and inches for height and stone or pounds for weight, which is very difficult for Chinese women to work out. For her benefit and by way of showing her you are thoughtful, please use centimeters ("cm") for your height and kilograms ("kg") for your weight. You can use a conversion website, e.g. http://www.convertit.com/Go/ConvertIt/Measurement/ Converter.ASP to convert the measurement.

7. Use correct English, fully spelt out

    If English is your native language, try to use it as correctly and fully as possible, avoiding non-standard usage and slang. Be aware that English is not her native language, and that you could also confuse her if you use incorrect English or abbreviations, e.g. "U" instead of "You", "lv" instead of "Love", "GSOH" instead of "Good Sense of Humor", "WLT" instead of "Would Like To" etc. Some Chinese women use translation software to help understand English, and the software cannot pick up these abbreviations. Please help her to understand you by using proper and simple English.

To further help you understand my suggestions on writing your profile, here for your reference are some good examples of profiles from our Asian Promise website:

I am a well-educated emotionally mature person. I have a passion about life, love, family and my work. I enjoy the fine arts, in fact, I enjoy the "fine" in everything. I am a willing patron of theatre, musicals, operas, concerts and interesting performances. I am fit. I enjoy light workouts, jogging. I ride, play golf, sail and enjoy travel. I am keenly educated into the Chinese culture. My favorite city in the world is Shanghai and after that…Vancouver. I am sincere and honest. I am looking for a life partner who is also intelligent, well educated, and emotionally stable. She wants to love and be loved. Hopefully we share some of the same interests and life passions. Happy optimistic disposition and family values would round it out nicely. I would make her life the happiest in the world.

I am a very unique man from New Zealand searching for his right woman. I am sweet natured, honest, loyal, playful, sexy, family oriented, down to earth, non-materialistic, not at all a player. I am very passionate, romantic and easygoing. I am looking for a woman that can commit to a long-term relationship. The person I'm looking for would enjoy spending as much time with me as I do with her. I want to think about that person during the day at work and be able to come home and look forward to seeing her that night. She should be someone that I'm proud to be holding hands with and tell everyone she is mine.

I live in the Northwest of America (Washington State). I am a fun and loving gentleman that is looking for the love of his life. I'm honest, trusting, trust-worthy and live life with integrity. I have a solid career based where I live and want to find the love of my life for the rest of my life. I want to have a wonderful relationship with my best friend. I'm looking for a beautiful Asian lady who is not only outwardly beautiful, but also has a beautiful heart. Someone I can share with and talk with and enjoys the outdoors. Eventually I would love to have a family together with as well.

I'm a man of 49 years old. I live in Genoa, town in the Northwest side of Italy. I work as therapist with people with mental disease. I am curious about other culture, about making experience to know better myself. I have traveled in many countries in the world and now I wish to dedicate my life to make a family. I'm looking for a sweet, easy-going, warm-hearted, passionate, home loving woman. We have to like each other and accept our culture differences, nay to transform them in positive resources for the relationship.

I am very easygoing, fun loving, adventurous, loving, faithful and honest. I am romantic and have a good sense of humor. I love animals and nature and enjoy walks in the country and travel to out of the way places. I have always had a great interest in China, its people and its culture. I believe Chinese ladies are beautiful and have so much to offer. I have recently visited Shenzhen and I loved it. I am now studying Mandarin and plan to visit again hopefully next year. I am looking for a lady who is loving, faithful, caring, energetic and healthy. She is serious about finding a soul mate who will love and treat her well. Not someone who is only looking for material gain.

2.3   Your photo

Adding a photo to your profile text will greatly increase the chances of finding your lover. This has been proven both by our experience and by that of others. Your photo means a lot more than just showing her your appearance. It means you are real, you are serious and you have nothing to hide from her. If a lady doesn't post her photo, she may have a good, understandable reason (it may prejudice friends, family or employers with conservative Chinese attitudes to know she divorced or is dating online). But if a man doesn't show his photo, his intention of finding a serious relationship would be questioned. Our experience shows that given two men with equally good profiles, most of our ladies prefer to contact the man with the photo.

It's better not to post a photo if you don't have a good one. Photos should be good or at least of reasonable quality, clear and pleasing. We understand that men may not be as good as women with photos, however some we receive are blurred, deformed or even roughly cut. To impress her, please dress neat and decent. You might want to look as you would when you're meeting a woman in person for a first date.

Don't try to impress her by showing a lot of skin. Sometimes we receive photos of men in swimsuits, thinking their muscular bodies make them masculine and sexy to her, but instead women are scared off. A friendly smile at her will be a big plus. One photo added to your profile is enough. Once you start to chat with her, you can exchange more photos to show your special interest for each other.

2.4 Your search

After posting your carefully prepared profile on the site you have researched and chosen, don't just wait for her to write or contact you. Be motivated and passionate enough to initiate your love search. It shouldn't be a difficult thing to do for men. However I would like to emphasize it here because it is important if you are looking for a Chinese or Asian bride.

1. Making the first move

    Most Asian ladies, including Chinese, are a little coy and like to be chased. As I said before, in the old days when marriage was arranged by parents, the man's parents would make the first approach to the lady's parents. Although things have changed, and most people now choose their life partner themselves, Chinese ladies still like the man to make the first move.

    Besides liking to be chased, Chinese ladies sometimes are not sure if it is a good or wise thing to do to contact men first. They are not so confident to take the first action. At my work I often receive letters from our ladies asking me:

    "Can I contact men first?"

"Do men like to be contacted by me first? Do men like women who make the initial move?"

"If I contact him first, does he think that I am too pushy or unwanted?"

"If I contact him first, does it make me less attractive?"

I have told ladies strongly that a lady making the first move is common in Western countries where being independent and confident can be attractive, and that this is different from being aggressive and pushy. However it will take time for them to adjust to this Western view. Men who write to the lady first will therefore always get a much better response than those who wait for the lady to make the first move.

2.   Don't give up

Mingli was divorced for one year before she joined Asian Promise. Soon she received many letters from men, but none of them interested her enough. She was still in the shadow of her divorce and didn't have confidence to find a new love even though she was longing for it.

Eventually she was touched by a man who had written to her again and again and told her that he was a good man. She replied to him and told him that she didn't believe in love. In the next two months he wrote to her continuously to help her gain confidence in life. When he flew from Australia to China to see her, Mingli was deeply moved and fell in love with him. His positive attitude and determination had eventually won her heart.

Here I didn't mean that you should be as persistent as Mingli's boyfriend. What I am saying is if you don't get a response from the lady that you wrote to, don't just give up. She may be testing how sincere you are and how much interest you have in her. As I noted above, Chinese ladies like to be chased. If she hasn't replied or said "no" to you, you always have room to try again. Keep writing to her and use the opportunity to show her your determination. If you think you are a good match and you have expressed it well in your emails, you will be rewarded in the end.

The more effort she can see from you, the more likely her heart will be touched. Don't just give up when she is still there for you!

3. More contacts mean a higher rate of success

    Dating statistics show that the more potential contacts you make the more chance you will have of being successful in finding love. This is particularly true if you are looking for Chinese or Asian love. Generally speaking Chinese or Asians are not as open as Westerners because they are shy about talking to strangers. It will take time for her to open up to you and for you to get to know her. Therefore, don't put all your hopes on one or two ladies but instead make good use of the Internet resource, which has brought you unlimited dating choices.

    After a wide search for an initial talk, we normally suggest you select two or three potentials for further chat. Over two to three months of chat with her, you will have a better idea if she is the right one for you and if she is the one you would like to see in person (I will discuss later the timing to see her in person). If your communication is good, by then your choice should be narrowed down to one. Meeting in person will serve only to further confirm your feelings about her.

2.5 Your first email

Your first communication is very important. Whether you can attract her attention or not will very much depend on what you write. Be sincere, honest and open. Let her feel that your email or letter is written just to her, not to just anyone.

From my work experience, I see that many men send their first letter/email to the lady without addressing her by name at the beginning. Some of the letters are long and romantic. However they are all about him with nothing about her. They are form letters only, written to a generalized woman, and the lady can't see his special interest in her.

Suggestions for Your First Email to Her

1. Be sincere, honest and open

2. Address her by name and spell it correctly

3. Tell her where you found her profile

4. Tell her why you are interested in her (use the information she wrote in her profile)

5. Further introduce yourself to her and reiterate what you are looking for in dating

6. Show your interest at her cultural background

7. Leave open questions (not just yes/no questions and answers) to create opportunities for further interactive communication

8. Keep your English as easy to understand as possible

It is important to use her name at the start of your email and tell her the reasons why you are interested in her. Since she is seriously looking for a life partner and a bit cautious about men playing games, your sincerity and particular interest in her are the keys to get her attention. All our ladies who have found true love told us they were initially touched by the sincerity of their lover.

In showing your sincerity to a Chinese lady, telling her something about your family is just as important as telling her about yourself—because your parents and siblings matter to Chinese. In addition, because the standard of living is still relatively poor in most places in China, financial status still plays an important role in marriage. It doesn't mean you need to tell her your income in your first email; however it is a good idea to let her feel financially secure.

Because of the different backgrounds and cultures in which you were raised, it is a good idea to let her know a bit about your lifestyle and habits. Tell her your general health, whether you are an evening or a morning person, whether you smoke or drink, if you are social or quiet, and so on. In addition, she will be very encouraged if you can show her your interest in her culture or show your determination to overcome the cultural or language barriers between the two of you.

I don't recommend you talk about politics, sex or other issues which are too heavy, sensitive or intimate in your first email. Make your first email warm, light and pleasant. You can discuss those topics with her later when you know her better. Finally, "True love" needs time, so don't ask her phone number and physical address in your first email.

If you take my advice in your first email to her, I can assure you that you will have a 90% chance of receiving a response. If you don't receive her reply immediately, don't panic! Some women don't have a connection at home and use Internet cafes instead, which they aren't able to do every single day. And some are still in the process of learning English, so some delays in response could be expected. Give her two or three days before you write to her again. Be prepared and take it easy if you receive a rejection. Chinese people believe in fate. A rejection doesn't always mean you are not good for her—it could simply mean your individual fates don't lie with each other. Bearing my advice in mind and continuing your search, you will find your fate eventually.

2.6   Meeting her in person

The following advice is from a gentleman who married a Chinese lady from our site.

"Please warn all your ladies: If he is not coming to see her after dating her online for six months, he is likely playing games or he is not financially qualified to date. This is only my personal advice and may not be correct. However I do think it is necessary to be more cautious when you date online."

I suggest meeting in person after dating online for two or three months (not more than six months). Although you can communicate via email, telephone, and webcam, these are still only semi-real means. Seeing is believing. Getting away from the computer screen and seeing her face to face is the only way to make yourself completely real to her, and to make her real to you.

If you meet too early, you may feel awkward or unconfident. To have good communication before you meet in person is a very wise and mature choice. From our experience, most men go to China to see their ladies after first corresponding with each other by email or telephone for two or three months. Of the couples that met in person after first spending this amount of time in online communication, 80% were married. However if you meet too late (more than six months), you may found you have wasted your time if the relationship doesn't work out. One of our couples had dated online for a year before seeing each other. After they found the relationship didn't work, they both regretted they hadn't met earlier.

Meeting her in person not only confirms your feelings towards her, but also shows your sincerity. If you don't have a really good reason to delay your trip to see her after six months of online dating, our experience shows your intentions will be strongly questioned—just as the gentleman said above.

I suggest there are many reasons you should visit her in China instead of her coming to your country for the first meeting:

- For her safety (don't insist her to go somewhere unfamiliar or a place which isn't public)
- To show your courtesy
- To show your sincerity
- To confirm your feelings about her
- Practical issues: it is difficult for her as a Chinese citizen to get a visa
- Money issues: most Chinese cannot afford an overseas trip
- To help you understand her by visiting her country and family
- To have a great trip to see ancient China today, with her as your personal guide

You need to consider her viewpoint. You are asking her to give up her job, home, family, culture and food to travel to a foreign country to live with someone she has only met through emails. This is a huge risk. And how does she know she will get along with you and will have security in the new place? Be an understanding and generous gentleman. Your effort will be rewarded. Here are the experiences of some real people on their first meeting in China:

"After emailing each other for a while we started to chat on MSN. I also called her every weekend. Five months later I flew to China to see her. A beautiful dream had finally become true."

"I met him in the airport yesterday. I recognized him as soon as he appeared. So did he. Everything was as expected. It has proved our wonderful feeling for each other."

"As I traveled for 17 hours on the plane, I got to know the flight attendants. They thought it was quite exciting about what I was doing. They told me that they had seen many people who as I was to meet someone they had met on the computer. They wished me luck and gave me a new full bottle of American wine for me to share with my new Chinese friends. They were all so nice to me and I enjoyed the flight very much. My adventure to China had really begun in earnest."

"The plane has landed and my heart is pumping fast. I keep asking myself: 'What if I don't recognize her? What if she doesn't like my look?' I come to the meeting point and quickly find her face in the crowd. She looks just as nervous as me. It is she! I leave my luggage on the floor and run toward her. We cuddle together and the nervousness is gone instantly. We are so happy to enjoy being together physically at last."

"I've got to say that it was everything and more of what I expected. She is, not only in her natural outward looks, but even more beautiful on the inside. I also met all of her family and they were very kind and generous to me throughout my stay, I enjoyed meeting them all. As I told you before leaving for Beijing I was very confident that she was the right one and the woman of my dreams, so I went prepared. I asked her to marry me. The trip gave both

of us the chance to confirm what we both already knew about each other with our daily conversations and emails to each other, and after finally meeting in person it just put any doubts to rest that we both had about each other."

"I arrived in Beijing. Somehow above all the noise from the airport, I heard the small sound of her voice calling my name. There she was, for real. She even looked cuter than her photo. For the entire nine days I was there, she brought me to see the Forbidden City, the Emperor's Summer Palace, the Temple of Heaven and the Lama Temple. I did go to the Great Wall of China. She made my dream come true. I met her family and her friends who all made me feel more than welcome in their homes. Just thinking about it now as I write this makes my heart feel so warm and grateful. They shared all they had and gave their love so freely and truly, so completely. I have never experienced such a wonderful trip before in my life. Mostly it was the Chinese people that I met who made my stay in China so wonderful. It was she who made my visit to China. She was the nicest of everyone there."

How romantic and wonderful they are! I wish I had those experiences with my husband Richard.

Some men have made their travel plans to see her after few months of correspondence with her, but as the travel departure date approaches he begins to get cold feet. If this is the case, meeting her in person may be exactly what you need. There is no question that meeting in person will help both of you clear up any doubts and worries, and will enable you to finally confirm your feelings for each other and seal the relationship. We suggest our ladies not make a commitment too soon, and that it is better to wait until you meet each other in person.

Preparing Your Trip to China

Airfare: Depends on your point of departure. Please ask your travel agent.

Hotel: US$30-100 (average) per night for range of 3-5 star hotels*

Food and local transportation: allow US$10-20 per day**

Tours: She will be pleased to offer you tour information/ service

Gift and souvenirs: recommend not more than US$100

Useful Links:

http://www.ebeijing.gov.cn/default.htm
http://www.ctsho.com/home_en040815/index.asp
http://www.expatsinchina.com/
http://www.alloexpat.com/china_expat_forum/

*For safety, I recommend you do not stay in hotels rated less than 3 stars. Hong Kong hotel rates are triple those in Mainland China.

**Food will be five times (rough estimate) as expensive in Hong Kong.

Indeed, it is a great opportunity to see China and finally meet the Chinese people. The place is historical, the culture is colorful and the people are very friendly. It is quite safe to travel in China if you follow standard safety advice for travelers. Stay in big cities or towns and don't go to undeveloped tour places where there are few or no people. Don't stop by beggars and listen to her advice. She will be your perfect "personal tour guide".

Make your trip to see her only

Peter dated Rose for four months online. They each decided the other was the one they had been looking for. Peter planned to fly from America to meet Rose in Sichuan, in western China. He wanted to prove his feelings before asking

Rose to marry him. However when Peter had first begun his search for love, he had also contacted Ying from Beijing. He was still keeping in touch with Ying as a friend at the time he decided to see Rose. He told Ying about his trip to Sichuan and made plans with Ying to meet her in Beijing after first seeing Rose there.

Peter was an honest gentleman. He made his plans clear to Rose, but she was confused and upset. Rose had been planing to show Peter around Beijing herself, but now Peter had arranged it with Ying. Peter flew to Sichuan to meet Rose, which was not so as good as they expected. A week later he left Sichuan and flew to Beijing to meet Ying. As I was expecting to hear good news about Peter and Rose, Peter called me from Beijing and told me that he was engaged to Ying. I was so surprised. That was only Peter's third day in Beijing!

Later after Peter returned back to America, he wrote me a long letter to explain why he had changed his mind. In the meantime I also received letters from Rose and Ying. Rose was sad and Ying was happy. I felt sorry for Rose but couldn't feel happy for Peter and Ying because it was too dramatic. However as faithful members of our website, I wished them everlasting happiness together.

Ying's fiancée visa application process took a year. During this time, Peter went back to Beijing to see Ying once more. As they got to know each other more and more, their relationship started to get shaky. At the last minute before the triumph of receiving the fiancée visa, Peter and Ying split. It didn't surprise me as much as their sudden engagement had.

Some men, who are seriously looking for a life partner, choose to see more than one lady on their trip to China. I understand this from the financial and time perspective. To make good use of the trip, they want to see more ladies in case one of them doesn't work out. It sounds like a wise choice, but unfortunately it doesn't work the way you would think. After all choosing a life partner is not like shopping around.

> The best way to reduce your risk in seeing one lady only
> is not by seeing others as well, but rather to have good
> communication with her before you meet her in person.
> Trust yourself. If you don't have faith in yourself, you'll lose
> her faith in you as well.

I encourage you to contact more ladies at the beginning of your search for initial chatting, but I recommend you make your trip to see one lady only. The best way to reduce your risk in seeing one lady only is not by seeing others as well, but rather to have good communication with her before you meet her in person (I will discuss good communication in the next chapter). This is why I suggest people do not meet too early, at least until you correspond with each other by email or telephone calls for at least two or three months.

As I said before, if you have both communicated well before you meet, your feelings are unlikely to change after meeting in person. Trust yourself. If you don't have faith in yourself, you'll lose her faith in you as well. Peter's experience is a good example.

3.   Wisely mastering your dating progress

I met Richard at Scottish Country Dance (SCD) in Hong Kong in 1998. Back then we were both working in Hong Kong, Richard was from the UK and I was originally from Beijing China (I had immigrated to New Zealand in 1991). The historical event of 1997 brought us to HK and SCD brought us to meet.

It was a Monday evening in spring. I danced as usual at the HK Cricket Club. Suddenly the music stopped and I found myself standing in front of a tall and handsome Western guy. As a SCD custom, we started to chat and Richard gave me a good impression of being polite and gentle. Richard told me that he had recently become a regular Monday dancer and I started to remember seeing him before. That evening passed quickly in our pleasant meeting and chatting. Before I left the dance for home, Richard invited me to a boat trip on the coming Saturday with his friends, but I excused myself because I get seasick.

Although I rejected Richard's invitation, I was looking forward to seeing him again on the next Monday dance. On Thursday, three days later, I received a fax from Richard at my work (he found my fax number from his friend in the dance). He listed four things for me to choose to go out with him. At that moment I felt he was being a bit pushy. However I gave myself a chance to know him better because I was alone in HK and needed to meet people. After all, he seemed to be a nice gentleman. I made a careful choice among the list. Ten days later, Richard and I went to a Welsh choir concert together.

We had a great time with Richard's friends at the concert and we all enjoyed the choir very much. That evening Richard and I also had chance to find more about each other. When I was telling him that I had a nine year old daughter, Richard almost spilt his beer on his shirt. He thought that I was younger than him and had never married before like him. However the surprise didn't stop him inviting me out. Over the next few weekends we spent time together doing mountain hikes, biking around the lake, having dim sum, Indian curry…In order to get know him more fully, I had my daughter or friends with us for some of the outings.

Due to my experience in the past, I was careful to develop my emotional closeness with Richard. I also thought the more serious we were, the slower we should take things. After two months dating him, I found myself attracted by his personality very much, which was the one that I was looking for in a life partner. However just as I felt ready to take a further step with him, Richard told me he had decided to go back to the UK. He hadn't seen the sparkle between us and felt there was no reason for him to remain in HK any more.

I was shocked and sad. I knew that we hadn't kissed each other like lovers, but my heart had been getting closer and closer to him. Apparently Richard hadn't noticed that. Several years of life experience in the West encouraged me to open myself up to him, which I couldn't imagine that I would do if I had always lived in China. I told Richard the reason I was taking the relationship *slowly and my intentions and feelings towards him. When I was telling him, I was so emotional and I was in tears.*

My heart touched Richard's heart, in a way Richard hadn't ever experienced before. He started to see a different kind of sparkle, which although didn't make his heart jump, instead made his heart warm and moved. Richard canceled his air ticket to the UK the next day and soon we had fallen deeply in love. That feeling was wonderful.

Men and women need to feel close to each other by both physical and emotional connections. However men tend to feel close physically, while women tend to feel close emotionally. Looking at the cultural aspect, where Westerners are dating for feelings and Chinese are dating for marriage, wisely mastering your dating progress with a Chinese lady is important to develop the potential of a lifelong happiness.

If you want to find a life partner, and not just a short-term relationship, prepare for it. Although it is harder and takes longer, it is nothing if you know what you will achieve later. All wonderful and valuable things come with hard work, including relationships. Please make the effort to allow her to get to know you. The more she knows you, the more sincerity she sees from you, the more feelings she will have for you.

> For most Westerners, physical contact is part of dating and it is perhaps very common to have sex after two or three dates. But for most Chinese ladies, physical contact is the result of dating progress and having sex is a kind of commitment to the relationship.

If you are both living in the same city and you meet her at work, a social event, or other ways locally, try to meet her again by inviting her out for concerts, dinners or parties from time to time (once a week for starters). Drinking is not a Chinese custom, so be careful if you invite her to go to bars.

When you take her out, try to create ways for her to get to know you better. For example, let her meet your friends or family members, find different topics to discuss through doing different activities, let her know your intentions towards her, introduce your culture step by step, tell her about your childhood and your interests, and ask her questions (very important to show your interest in her).

Give her time to develop her feelings as she becomes more familiar with you. Don't be too quick to judge her attachment based on physical contact. For most Westerners, physical contact is part of dating and it is perhaps very common to have sex after two or three dates. But for most Chinese ladies, physical contact is the result of dating progress and having sex is a kind of commitment to the relationship. Because of this, if you are not sure about your relationship with her, be careful about having sex with her. Otherwise you may mislead her (I'll discuss this more in the next section).

If you meet her online or if you live far away, you are in a better position to focus on knowing each other through chat. Don't meet her too early, but instead make good use of the geographical distance to first get to know each other's thoughts. If you meet online I suggest you communicate via email at the beginning. After one month's initial chatting, you should know whether the two of you have similar intentions and views on the main things in life. This is important for you to decide whether to carry on with her or to stop. If you carry on, your next step would be to develop feelings for each other over the next few months. Besides email, you can use online chatting, telephone, video and webcams, and mail letters and gifts to each other.

If all goes well you can meet her in person after a few months of Internet chat. By then you both should have quite a good feeling for each other. The meeting is just a way to confirm your feelings. Don't ask her to remove or turn off her profile at any time—leave it to her to decide. Trust her by trusting your feelings about her.

Suggestions for a Long Distance Relationship (LDR)

1. Be prepared for it—be responsible for your choice

2. Have a good foundation for love—sincerity, honest, trust, respect and commitment

3. Keep up good communication—reassure her that she is continually loved

4. Try to live together ASAP and meanwhile meet with her as many times as you can

5. Keep a positive attitude in managing your lives without each other

6. Plan your future together—reunion plans, marriage plans, family plans...

7. Find support from others who are in LDRs (see www.candleforlove.com)

8. Believe in yourself and your love—love can overcome many difficulties!

Whether you meet online or offline, and assuming both parties begin with the intention of developing a marriage relationship, it normally takes two or three months time to get to know and develop feelings for each other ("love at first sight" excepted). A "real love", not just lust, needs time indeed. Nowadays with the various forms of IT communication available, we don't find much difference in dating timelines between short and long distance relationships. However it does depend on the people involved. At least two to three months time is needed, and it is not at all surprising for some to need longer.

Expect your dating to be full of the usual mixture of happiness, sadness, inspiration and desperation that you would find in any dating in which both couples are investing their energy, but with the added challenges of language and cultural differences. While many of our men would say Chinese wives are absolutely among the best choices available to the Western world, this doesn't mean they are waiting to bring lifelong happiness to you. The happiness comes only with your efforts in being patient, persistent, and committed, plus a great deal of determination, compromise and understanding, which are all the essentials for the foundation of a real and lifelong love.

4.   Sex

Like most women, Chinese ladies enjoy sex with someone they love and feel safe with. Sex is the ultimate form of love. Many Chinese ladies choose to date Western men because they think Westerners are gentle, caring and respectful in sex and do not base it solely on physical needs. All of the men who responded to my survey in late 2004 [3] agreed that good sex is very important for relationships and marriage, and they all cared about their lovers' feelings regarding sex. Chinese ladies will very much appreciate your keeping these attitudes.

> Many Chinese ladies choose to date Western men because they think Westerners are gentle, caring and respectful in sex and do not base it solely on physical needs.

4.1   Attitudes on sex before marriage

According to research done in the late 80's in Beijing [4], about 30% of women were accepting of sex before marriage. This was a huge change and would have been unheard of prior to the 80's. Nowadays, I believe, the majority of educated women in China accept sex before marriage if they feel loved. However there are still many Chinese women restricted by traditional thought who maintain their virginity or avoid sex until after marriage. Having sex before marriage would make them feel guilty, ashamed or taken advantage of.

Although society does have an influence, it is still basically up to her whether she accepts or refuses sex before marriage. Compared to the past, modern society is much more relaxed and generous about the issue. If a woman refuses to have sex prior to marriage or a man insists on marrying only a virgin, this is due more to his or her personal values rather than to external pressures.

Love is powerful. Although she may still be influenced by the old traditions, your love, respect and assurance could change her attitude.

4.2   What does sex mean to Chinese women?

Because of their background of traditional beliefs, having sex means a great deal to Chinese women. For them, sex is an end result of the dating process. If you have sex with her too soon, it could lead her to think:

1. You are not a serious person and just want sex with her, or
2. You love her and intend to marry her.

So if you are serious about the relationship, or if you are not ready to commit, it is wise not to rush to have sex with her, whether she would accept it or not. Moreover, don't judge her feelings about you based on how soon she has sex with you. Please take the time for her to know you and feel loved and valued by you, as these are the most effective ways for her to accept and enjoy being with you physically.

To most Chinese women, having sex is the result of love and is a kind of commitment to the relationship. It is a serious thing and it is not just for fun or physical need.

4.3   Can I discuss sex with her?

Yes, you can. Although Chinese women are more shy than Western women when it comes to sex, your lady will be more than happy to discuss it with you if she can see it benefits you both. After all, talking about personal attitudes and expectations regarding sex in relationships and marriage is different from talking about sex organs and sexual positions, as the latter are driven purely by eroticism.

Many Chinese ladies I have talked to had uncertain or confused feelings on their Western boyfriend's sexual intentions and expectations. They didn't know how they should react if he were to ask to have sex. Be open and let her know your intentions and your thoughts about sex, as this will help her understand you and open up to you as well. Good communication about sex will make both of you relax and enjoy being together more.

It is also sensible to talk about sexual health concerns. We understand that getting too practical may lessen the romance; however your health is the most important thing in your life. Luckily AIDS and STDs are not so common in Chinese women. However the media has given Chinese the impression that there is a high incidence of AIDS and STDs in the West. So it is in your best interest to allay her concerns by raising the subject and clearing the clouds. Doing so not only shows your concern for your own health, but also shows your concern for her.

4.4   Practical issues

Chinese ladies tend to be fairly traditional around sex, and when first getting to know you may not be comfortable with some of the more liberal suggestions on the place and manner of having sex. If you meet online, on your first visit to see her in person be a gentleman and book separate rooms. After you feel more comfortable with each other, you will quite likely end up sleeping together, but you must just take things as they go. Don't ruin a lifetime of potential because you think you are ready to sleep together before she does.

If you are not sure or haven't had a chance to talk with her about sexual health issues, use a condom when having sex. Don't assume that because she hasn't said "No", it means she accepts having sex without a condom. She may be too shy to say it, or she may not be aware of the risks (sex education in China is not as good as it is in the West). Both of you will feel much more relaxed about having sex without having to think about all these risks while you're being intimate with someone for the first time.

Wearing a condom is also a reasonable protection against pregnancy. Chinese women are quite fertile and contraception should not be based on the time of the month approach (the rhythm method), or ignored altogether. Chinese ladies may not be as against abortion as others (abortion is common because of China's one child policy), but you may feel uncomfortable about it, or may feel guilty and that you have to marry her even though you are not ready.

5. Money

Spending money on a Chinese lady is still an important way to show your intentions. This stems from the old tradition, but is different than dating or marrying for money. In the old days, as I said in Chapter One:

"The man's family would take the initial action on the marriage and, after the arrangement was agreed by both sets of parents, would send engagement presents to the woman's family. This was a symbol that the man's family had purchased their daughter as a bride from the woman's family."

Splitting the bill on social occasions is becoming more acceptable in China, but is still not done outside the big cities, and definitely not for dating. On a date, men are still expected to pay for dinners, shows and other expenses. If you use the Western way and wait for her to decide whether or not to pay or share the cost, she won't understand it as your respect of her right to choose. Instead she will take it as evidence you are stingy or don't love her. She will pay you back in other ways such as inviting you to her home for dinner, buying you presents, looking after you, etc. Although it is becoming more popular to share the cost of the wedding, there is still the traditional influence of the expenses being borne mainly by the groom.

Generally speaking, most Chinese ladies still see money as proof of your intentions and your love. A Chinese lady will expect you to spend money on her not because she is greedy, but instead because she wants to see how much you love her. If you don't have money, it will be different. She will help you save money and even offer you financial help, if she loves you. Please understand that although she may be happy to see you spending money on her, she won't say so. She also won't tell you directly when she needs your financial help. She expects you to figure this out and she believes that if you love her, you will realize her need.

I have frequently explained to our ladies that in the West money is not the only measure of love, and that sharing the cost shows independence and respect. I also tell them:

"Be open and direct if you need him to help financially. Western men don't use money to win a lady's heart as Chinese men do. However if he can see that you need money and if he loves you, he will be more than happy to help you as much as he can."

Chinese ladies are still in the process of learning the modern approach. Please understand your lady's attitude, and give her time to accept a way of thinking more commonly seen among today's Western women.

6.   Precautions

China has been developing very quickly, and the lives of the people have been much improved over the last few decades. In my years of experience, I have found that most ladies are not focused on looking for money or for a way to leave China. What they are doing is looking for love.

For example, although the single, lifelong marriage of the past has become history, there still remain some old Chinese thoughts deeply rooted in thousands of years of tradition. For example, Chinese men are reluctant to accept previously married ladies, particularly so if they have a child. Unfortunately, Chinese women suffer greatly from the effects of these old ways of thinking. Ladies are therefore turning to us to help them to find love with Westerners, who put one's values and personality first.

Of course, people are people everywhere. Some are good and some are not. Some look for true love and some look for something else. Just like some women anywhere in the world, there are some Chinese women who want money or a foreign passport and will use Western men to get them (in general, the quality of life in developed countries is still much better than most places in China). Those women are different from the women who want to improve their quality of life through true love and marriage. They are selfish and are not interested in love, but only in money.

Learn as much as you can before you fall in love. There is no substitution for good communication as a way to check out each other's sincerity (I will discuss communication issues further in the next chapter). Look for clues and ask questions using your common sense.

Watch For the Following Red Flags:

1. Overemphasizing her youth and beauty
2. Only being interested in your money and property
3. Falling in love with you too quickly
4. Being keen on expensive things
5. Making you feel you are being pushed or seduced
6. Always having reasons to ask more money from you
7. Showing off your wealth to her friends or family, instead of your love
8. Not trying hard to communicate with you by seriously attempting to learn English
9. Using an agency instead of communicating online with you directly
10. Acting inconsistently, dishonestly or too nice to be true
11. Anything else that makes you feel doubtful or uncomfortable—trust your gut instincts

More warnings:

Chinese Dating and Marriage Agencies/Brokers

There are many money-minded Chinese dating and marriage agencies/ brokers in China. They make their money by using people who want to get out of China or who are naive. Their customers normally speak little or no English and come from poor remote areas of China. The agencies charge enormous sums of money (roughly equivalent to two year's salary) in return for guarantees to find a foreign husband for them. Nowadays more and more agencies in China are starting to use the Internet to find foreign husbands for their customers. They divide their service into three stages and charge their customers at each stage: finding/writing fee, meeting fee and success/marriage fee. The agencies look for dates and communicate with the dates on behalf of their customers. The agencies don't tell their customers the contact details of the men they are dating so that they can control the whole dating progress.

Many foreign men who have met ladies on the Internet are blind to the truth. When they finally meet their lover they find she is not the one they have corresponded with over the months, and discover her knowledge of English is very poor. Because there was actually no real communication, they find therefore there is no real love. Most such relationships through agencies, sooner or later, fail.

I often hear stories from men like the following:

I arrived with the expectation that she knew some English and have discovered that she speaks virtually no English. She was using a friend from her city to speak with me on the phone and did not tell me this beforehand, so when I arrived I was much disoriented.

A "friend" here is normally the agent, whose services she pays for.

Dating and marriage agencies/brokers, in general, do not have a good name in China. We sincerely suggest you do not use them. If you don't have an opportunity to meet your lady where you are, the Internet is a great way to find her. However if you do find her through the Internet, make sure you are communicating with the lady herself and not an agent or a "friend". It is not difficult for you to find out the truth if you are aware bad agencies do exist in China. To avoid being cheated by dishonest dating agencies or ladies when you date on the Internet, I suggest:

1. To use the dating sites where the Chinese ladies come to the site themselves directly and not to use the dating sites where the Chinese ladies are from indirect sources, e.g. local dating and marriage agencies/brokers, translators, "friends" or others.

2. To test the identity of the person you're communicating with by using a web camera. If your lady is able to access the Internet, she is able to install a webcam that costs much less than a computer.

3. That whether her English is good or not is not so important. The more important thing is her attitude to English. If she continues to use a translator to communicate for her and doesn't study and practice English hard herself, her sincerity to find true love is questioned (I will come back to this issue again in the next chapter). Love needs good communication, of which a common language between you plays an important role in your future happiness.

It is the bad practice of local dating and marriage agencies/brokers who have planted the seeds for bad and sad stories that have happened before and are still happening now. This is also the reason why Chinese government is always cautious about international dating and marriage. Chinese government wants to avoid the bad stories happening by controlling those agencies' practice. This is the same in the US, where the US Government introduced very strict laws (IMBRA) governing international marriage brokers and dating service and sites in March 2006. However "To give the sword to people" is the most effective way to help people find true love and to stop someone using people's ignorance to make money.

Biased Media

People are often misled by the media. Does the following story sound familiar?

David was genuinely seeking the love of an Asian woman. He found her, brought her to the USA, and got married. As soon as she became a permanent resident, she filed for divorce.

It's the same for Chinese, as we often hear stories like the following from Chinese newspapers:

Ming married her American husband one year ago. When she decided to marry him, all her friends and family members disagreed. Ming insisted to marry him. Just a few months after she got married, she found her husband was violent. He often came back home late after drinking. If she complained, he would beat her. He spent all his money on himself and left her no money.

…they sell their Chinese wives for money after they bring them to their countries. Those women end up having to work as prostitutes…

A distorted image of reality is caused by the longstanding history of barriers between China and the first world, and because the media is often used for political purposes. Although we know unfortunate things do happen everywhere, anytime and in any race in the world, we still get confused after being told again and again the bad things rather than the good. It is wonderful to see the prejudices fading as the barriers wash away. Trust yourself with your own sense and observations. Don't go with others without thinking carefully. Ask yourself:

"If there are always bad endings, how do you explain the thousands of happy Asian/Sino-Western couples in the world?"

There is always some risk in anything, and finding a cross-cultural love is no exception. It is said that the bigger the risk the greater the reward. But the question is not about the extent of risk; the question is whether you want to have a true love. If you want it, you have to take the risk and there is no other option. However you can reduce your risk by using your wisdom, stemming from your own life experience, and by taking steps to educate yourself more on the subject. This book serves exactly that purpose. It helps you to reduce the risk so that you will enjoy more the beauty of a Chinese love.

Reference

[1] Survey of female Asian Promise members conducted in November 2003. More than 100 women participated.

[2] Connecting You to Love/Finding True Love Online—written by Li Xiao Yan and published by Cosmos Books (Hong Kong)/China Youth Press (Mainland China).

[3] Email survey of 50 Western men from our Asian Promise website, ranging between 30 and 60 years of age (survey performed late 2004).

[4] Love and Sexuality of Chinese Women—written by Li Yin He and published by China Today.

Chapter 4 How to Communicate Well

> You know what they say about investing in property—if
> you want to be successful, then the most important thing is
> 'location, location, location'. When it comes to relationships
> there is a secret for success as well, and that secret is 'commu-
> nication, communication, communication'.
>
> Sally Taylor Jensen, Author of "The Secrets of Love"

Indeed, communication is the key to a successful relationship. Love comes
from sincerity, understanding, respect, closeness, trust and commitment,
which are all based on good communication.

Many people blame their relationship failure on their differences, and
particularly so in the case of a cross-cultural relationship with its additional differences in culture and language. But they don't realize that love
can overcome many differences and difficulties, if the love includes good
communication. If a person doesn't communicate well, he or she won't be
successful in any sort of relationship.

It is true that a cross-cultural relationship can be more challenging.
The reason, however, is not because of wider differences between the
people, but rather because of the higher requirement for communication.
There are many books teaching people how to develop good communication skills, but here I will focus only on those which help you to connect
your heart to Chinese ladies.

> Love can overcome many differences and difficulties if the love includes good communication. If a person doesn't communicate well, he or she won't be successful in any sort of relationship.

1.   Sincerity and Honesty

Kevin, a software developer said:

"Communication is what keeps a relationship going. It is by far the most important thing. Honesty sits right up there too. If you aren't being honest (with yourself and each other) then it isn't really a relationship."

Susan Tong, one of our ladies, said:

"If you are looking for a life partner, you must be sincere and serious because you are aiming for your own lifelong happiness. Your partner would only be sincere to you if you are sincere to them."

In the first section of Chapter 3 ("Your honesty wins her honesty") I addressed this issue as it pertains to clarifying your dating intentions. Certainly, your approach to dating will heavily influence your attitude towards communication.

No matter which culture you are from, it is agreed that a good marriage is based on a real, meaningful relationship. Such a relationship is possible only with sincere communication, the bedrock foundation of a true love. With sincerity, when differences and difficulties arise, both parties have the courage and the desire to bring them to the table; they are willing to listen and understand; they are able to work it out. Their sincere intent in communication will bring closeness, understanding, respect and affection all round. The true communicator creates a safe and open climate for both people, allowing the couple to face challenges together.

Meng met Dave a few years ago and now they are married and live in the USA. When they first began getting to know each other, Meng had many questions about Dave's past and their future together. Here is one of her letters:

"Although I only met you a few weeks ago, I can tell you are a serious and honest man, which is very important to me. Because of my bad experience in the past, I want to take time for us to know each other more and more. Do you mind to answer me the following questions?:

You said that your ex-wife was a good person, then why did you get divorced? Why did she take everything owned by two of you? I don't under-stand them. May be it is from our different culture. Do you think love can exist with different cultures?"

The next day Meng received Dave's reply:

"I don't mind answering your questions. It is the way we will get to know each other. I got divorced because my ex-wife didn't like that I had to go to Korea for my military commitment. So when I left, we got divorced a short time after I left. I didn't fight the divorce so she got all the property and vehicle that was left at the house. I was sad about it but to be bitter would be wasted energy. I try to think good thoughts. When I said she was a good woman, I do not want to hold a grudge against her.

To me, your last question is the most important. Yes, I do. I wouldn't have started talking to you if I didn't feel it could work out. It is not an easy process to love someone from a different culture, but if two people really love each other they can make it work. There has to be give and take from both sides. I have seen many happy families with parents from different cultures. I know I have the ability and compassion to adapt and want to love that special lady."

Your sincerity and determination may truly be challenged because of the difficulties of cross-cultural and/or long distance dating. Don't be dis-heartened! Our experience shows that people who have chosen this path are generally more mature and are more likely to achieve a successful relationship.

2.   Openness

2.1   Be clear about your intentions

As explained before, because of traditional influences the majority of Chinese ladies nowadays are still dating with marriage as the goal. It will benefit both of you to be straightforward about your reasons for dating. I recently received this letter from one Chinese lady:

> *"I have been to your website and I like it very much. I want to join as a member to find a Western husband because I like its culture. But my recent experience has set me back. He was from Holland and he was teaching English in my home city. I met him from my friend. He was nice and gentle. We dated for a month before he returned to his country. We had a good time together. I fell in love with him. I have introduced him to my parents under his request. He promised to write to me after he returns home. But he never writes to me and I haven't heard from him for two months since he left. My heart is broken. I lost my faith in Westerners now and I am too scared in case it happens to me again. Can you help me?"*

It was sad. However it is hard for me to say if he was a cheater or he just wanted a short term relationship. If he just wanted a short term relationship, this kind of behavior might be understandable from a Western point of view but it wasn't right for most Chinese.

As more and more Westerners are now working in China, we have seen an increase in similar stories. It is good that East can meet West at a personal level today, but if care is not taken, it can increase the obstacles stemming from different cultural views. For example, she may think you are inviting her out for dinner or a movie because you are interested in marriage. When it turns out it just is for a good time or a short term relationship, she may feel cheated and think you are a game player. She thinks "like" equals "love" because Chinese lovers are often too shy to say "I love you". When it turns out completely different, she feels confused. These different views have resulted in some myths among Chinese regarding Western attitudes towards love and marriage.

I frequently explain to our ladies that Westerners have different terms for dating, although they are all based on love, and I also explain the difference between "like" and "love". However the best way to avoid misunderstanding and confusion is to be completely open to each other. Tell her what kind of relationship you are looking for right up front and then continue to be honest about your feelings. Be aware of the differences and respect each others choices. Don't forget that sometimes your reasons for dating can change over time. Keep up your good communication with her and be honest about your feelings at all times, remembering she is likely to be too shy to ask you. Although she may be upset by changes in your feelings, your openness and honesty can help her to accept them positively.

2.2　Explore each other's values and expectations

When you start to date someone, no matter whether you meet them on or offline, you always have questions: "Is she my Miss Right? Am I her Mr. Right?" When dating someone from a different culture or background, you may have additional concerns such as:

"Are we able to overcome the cultural differences? Does she want to move to my country? Does she want to use me to get a foreign passport, or money? What does she expect from me? Would she work hard to make our marriage work in the future?…"

She may worry:

"Is he honest and really looking for marriage, or is he just a game player? Will he be nice and treat his future wife respectfully? Can he accept my child? Will he support me in a new country? Will he mind my Chinglish? (English with Chinese flavor)…"

All of these concerns are very important for both of you. Remember you are looking for a lifelong partner and therefore her life values and expectations must be close to yours. We understand that everyone is different and it is impossible to find someone who is exactly the same as you. But having similar values and close expectations on the main issues in life will not only ease the difference, but will also turn that difference into challenge and excitement. Otherwise, without agreeing on the main issues, the relationship can be an ordeal.

Some put feelings first and believe in love at first sight. Some even fall in love at the click of a mouse. I am not against the feeling of love at first sight, but I do think a mature person conducts his lifelong relationship in a careful and well thought out manner. Many couples become unhappy or divorced not from the change in each other later in the relationship, but from the difference that existed right from the start. A good and real love needs a solid foundation. Have good communication on the important issues before you fall in love, and don't leave yourself in a dilemma later.

The best, quickest and most effective way to find out whether you are right for each other is to ask questions on the main issues that concern you. From the answers you also can see your prospective partner's sincerity and seriousness, like Meng and Dave's communication above. Below I list some suggested questions. In my Chinese language book [1] I also suggested similar questions for Chinese ladies to ask you.

Suggested Questions on Values and Expectations

1. What are your spiritual beliefs?

2. What are your values and how do you prioritize them?

3. What things are important in a relationship/marriage?

4. What is your expectation for your future husband?

5. What type of husband do you like—A hard worker? Family-minded?…

6. Why do you want to find a Western husband in particular?

7. What is your picture or expectation of life in the West?

8. Do you prefer to live in the city or the country? What do you imagine life will be like in the countryside in the West?

9. Are you willing to move to a new country and accept a new life?

10. Do you think that love can exist with different cultures and backgrounds?

11. How do you feel about having a family? Do you want children? If so, how many?

12. Do you support or live with your children? Are you close to them?

13. What are your plans for yourself and your children after you get married again?

14. Are you willing to work or do you prefer to stay at home?

15. What does romance mean to you and how important is it?

16. Are you willing to talk about sex and its importance in a relationship?

17. How good is your relationship with your extended family (parents and siblings)?

18. Where do your parents live? Do you see them often? Do they know you are dating Westerners? How would they feel about that?

19. Do you have many friends? What does friendship mean to you?

Basically you can use Western ways to ask Chinese ladies any question without worrying too much about cultural offenses, as long as you do it politely and with respect. However you should also be prepared for her questions about your age, health or income as well as similar information about others. These are not considered personal questions ("it's not your business!") in Chinese culture as they are in the West. If you're not comfortable answering any particular question, please respectfully explain your culture to her. You can also answer in a different way. For example if you don't want to tell her your income, you can still give her an idea of your quality of life by telling her about your goals, lifestyle, hobbies, etc. Don't just assume her question means she is interested only in your money. As I have noted, Chinese ladies want to feel financially secure in the marriage, and in China one's income is still the only or main financial source.

When you do ask questions, please make them as easy as possible for her to understand. Don't ask her too many questions at once, which at the beginning may put too much pressure on your relationship or on her limited English. You can split up some questions and ask them step by step as things go and develop. The questions listed above are just my suggestions for your reference. If you have your own particular concerns, please do ask her about them. In the meantime, help her to ask you questions as well.

2.3   Encourage her to ask you questions and tell you her concerns

Chinese ladies are shyer and less confident talking about themselves and what they think than are Western ladies. Asking her questions will help you get to know her. However she will probably still feel shy about telling you what she wants to know and what her concerns about you are.

Because of their long history of subordinate status, Chinese ladies may not have a strong awareness of what they want, nor much confidence to achieve it. Although Chairman Mao did give Chinese women equal rights as men, he didn't give them the right to think for themselves and do what they want. To please others and do what is expected is still the natural behavior for many Chinese ladies.

In dating a Chinese lady, you have a unique responsibility to help and encourage her to think and speak for herself. As you know, it is very important for the future health of your relationship. To be successful in this special role, I suggest the following:

- Let her know that you are attracted by her personality and are not concerned about her age, her appearance or the fact that she has been previously married or already has children.

- Let her know that you believe in true and long-lasting love, and that they require good communication.

- Tell her that if she's not happy, you won't be happy.

- Explain that you respect her concerns and will try to understand her point of view even though yours may differ.

- Promise that you will ask her if you have any questions and concerns.

- Show appreciation for her questions that have helped or will help the two of you get to know each other more deeply.

Nowadays more and more Chinese ladies have started to learn to think for themselves, but they still lack confidence to speak out. No doubt your Western attitudes of independent thinking and assertiveness will encourage her to stand up for herself. With your help, Chinese women will strive to find the real meanings of "true love" and "equal rights".

2.4   Tell her your concerns or worries

Discussing the main issues at the beginning of the relationship will help you decide whether to pursue it further or not. However as the depth of the relationship develops, it is still quite common for people to begin to feel uncertain. This is a sign of a healthy maturity, the place where the realities of true love supplant the initial illusions of falling in love. Please remember: A good marriage requires true love, and true love requires honesty. Being honest and open is the best way to ease your apprehensiveness. Here is one American gentleman's experience:

"I know many Chinese ladies who think Americans are rich and have an easy life. When I was dating Bing, I was very honest with her about my financial status and even showed her my bank statement at the end of each month. There wasn't much left. I wanted her to know that I wasn't rich and I needed to work hard. I wanted her to prepare for it and not to be disappointed when she joins me from China later."

Many Westerners are concerned the lady may be looking for money or a passport, not for real love. You should clear this up with her at the beginning of the relationship. If you are still worried after you fall in love with her, you need to let her know.

To avoid upsets or misunderstandings, I suggest you explain well the reasons behind your concerns. This is one of the important communication skills for people from different cultural backgrounds to know and learn. Letting her know your reasons will help her understand your concerns and worries from your point of view. I will come back to this important skill later.

2.5   Tell her if you want to stop

If you are no longer interested in communicating with her, don't just "fall off the face of the earth" or not say anything and leave her in the dark. Please be respectful and polite. When you are communicating via email or online chat, keep in mind that on the other end she is a real person with real feelings.

Also, if you don't want to date her any more, please tell her the truth and don't mislead her or leave her hanging. Some men try to be kind and don't want to upset the lady. They still keep in touch with her or find an indirect excuse. Please see the examples below:

1)   *He changed his mind after he promised to marry her. He kept telling her that he still loved her but needed more time to think. First he asked her to wait for him for one month and after that he asked her to give him another three months to think. In the meantime, he still kept in touch with her but with less and less communication. His unclear message drove her crazy. She sent emails to him 3 times a day and only got a reply every 2-3 days. She didn't know what she should do—wait or forget him? She loved him so much that it made her life very difficult and she became depressed. She wanted to see him and get a real feeling from him, but he was living thousands of miles away.*

2) *He met her on the Internet. He changed his mind after meeting her in person. According to the lady, they had a good time together when he was in China. He even said that he would apply for her fiancée visa as soon as he returned home. However as soon as he did return home, he sent her a letter and told her that his children opposed the marriage. He said that his children were his first priority, so he had to give up the idea of marrying her. It was a big surprise to the lady. She ended up blaming it on the Western culture, and came to believe that in the West people are not serious about relationships and there is no long-lasting love.*

For goodness sake, please tell her the truth. "Short pain is better than long pain". Although it may be difficult to accept at the beginning, it is best for her in the long run. As cross-cultural and long distance relationships are more challenging, being honest is even more important. If you leave her in confusion or misunderstanding, it could cause more harm for her in the future. If it is difficult to tell her face to face or on the phone, write her a letter to explain your true thoughts.

In our experience, ladies who have been treated honestly and respectfully have a much more positive attitude towards the failure of a relationship, and have a much better ability to use lessons learned towards future success.

3   Be aware of differences in background

We all know men and women have different perceptions and different ways of acting. It is very important to understand these differences in order to have a good relationship and marriage. Moreover, your views and behaviors are affected by how and where you grew up. If you date a lady who is from a different culture or country, be aware of the difference and be careful not to judge her based on your own background experience and knowledge. Communicating well and trying to understand one another from the other person's point of view are important keys to a successful cross-cultural love.

3.1   Don't prejudge her without being sure you have communicated correctly

One night, soon after I fell in love with Richard, we went to the cinema in Causeway Bay. After the movie, we didn't want to leave each other and came to a quiet bar nearby. The movie had made us feel very much in love. Our thoughts flowed from the screen romance to ourselves. Richard ordered a beer and I had a cup of coffee. Richard looked deep in my eyes and said with sincere affection:

"I have a concern about our future. Compared to your ex-husband [he had died two years prior] I am much younger and have less life experience. I am worried that I am not as good as he to bring the love that you and your daughter expect. I am worried that I will disappoint you."

I felt my body instantly sink from a loving river to an ice hole. My immediate reaction was that Richard was hinting to me to hold back on our relationship. My brain went blank and I could not think or respond to Richard, who was desperately waiting for my feedback. Soon, surprised by my response, Richard too was shaken off track. We both sat in the bar in silence. An intimate night finished in numbness.

I couldn't sleep that night after I got home. After struggling the whole night, I finally decided to accept his hint. I called Richard and invited him out for lunch in the morning. At the lunch table I held back my sobs and told him that we should stop. Richard didn't say anything and sat there like a log. When I returned his book and he gave me my key back, I felt my whole life coming to an end.

I was so sad that I had to cancel my duty to teach a Chinese lesson that night. Scott was my student and good friend. When I told him that I was too sad to teach, he kindly invited me out to have a talk. Scott was an American guy in his late thirties and had been working in Hong Kong for a few years. After I told him the details of my drama with Richard, Scott said:

"I think your judgement was wrong. Richard didn't mean to leave you; instead he loves you and cares very much for you and your daughter. I have

friends from China and Korea and understand that Asian men don't share their feelings with their partners. Although he may have lots of worries or concerns at home or work and needs someone to share them with and give him support, he has to hide these problems and pretend to be a big strong man. Otherwise he would be treated as a loser and looked down on by others. Whereas in the West, we advocate openness and sharing. Everyone needs help and support. Richard wanted to share his feelings with someone he felt close to. If you love him, you should share his feelings and ease his concerns by encouraging and reassuring him."

It turned out Scott was right. Soon Richard and I were happily back together. Indeed, Scott ended up giving me a lesson instead of the other way round. It was such a valuable lesson that it saved me from losing a life-long happiness. I learned I had wrongly judged Richard using the Chinese way of thinking. I forgot Richard and I were from different backgrounds and we had different views on certain things. Of course Richard learned a lesson too. He learned that he should explain in depth the reasons behind his concerns if he talks to someone from a different background. From then on, we always made sure our messages came across correctly. Good communication became a key to our happy relationship.

This story is based on the man's concern being prejudged by the lady. However the same pattern can happen where her concern is prejudged by him. In any situation, be aware of the difference in backgrounds and don't judge each other without first making sure you have communicated correctly. You may not be as lucky as I was in getting timely help from an "expert", so help yourself by keeping up your good communication with her. If you are not sure what she is talking about, please ask her to explain, and in the meantime, try to learn as much as possible about her background and culture.

3.2   Be careful on some particularly sensitive issues

To help you understand Chinese ladies and avoid misunderstandings, there are some issues I would like to go through with you. These issues are sensitive and could unnecessarily ruin your potential relationship, and therefore I suggest you do not discuss them until you know her quite well (e.g. already know her values and expectations).

1. Politics

We know there is a big political difference between the West and China, and particularly between the USA and China. The different political environments mean the government and the media may portray the same events differently in one country than in the other. Therefore sometimes a dating couple's conflicting opinions stem not so much from divisions in their deeply held personal beliefs, but rather from various biased political agendas. Here are some examples from my experience:

One lady had a big argument with her boyfriend on their attitudes towards the Japanese, which made them both very upset. One loving couple separated because of the Iraq war. After watching a movie about the AIDS problem in the USA, another lady asked her American boyfriend about his views on AIDS. He felt offended and pointed the finger back at her: "China, in fact, has the fastest increasing incidence of AIDS." Her question almost put their relationship to death.

Again, be aware of your different backgrounds. Although you may not reach agreement, be understanding and respectful. Your similar values on the main life issues will lead you to the same path with time. Don't let politics control your relationship and your life.

2. Religion

As explained in Chapter 2, Mao's elimination of all culture and religion left Chinese women a blank slate and thus open-minded in many ways. Although they have their own beliefs, more than 90% of Chinese do not subscribe to any particular organized religion. Thus they are free from the constraints of religious rules; they can divorce and remarry, choose to have an abortion (in fact, abortion is common because of the one child policy in China), and marry anyone they wish without regard to religion.

If your lady doesn't have religious beliefs, please don't assume that she is not keen on spiritual nourishing. Many Chinese have become religious after they move to the West.

3. Law and regulations

    Western people grow up in an environment of a well-established system of law. From the time they are very young, they are educated to obey the laws and follow the regulations. Everyone, whether ordinary citizen, premier, prime minister or president, has equal rights and justice before the law.

    Things are very different in third world countries like China. The system of law and the regulations are not so organized or well-established. And even where the rules may make a bit of sense, the law only applies to some. The laws work more or less for you depending on your social level and how powerful you are. It has become a necessary skill for people to learn to work around the law and the regulations. The higher your skill in this regard, the more likely you are to get ahead of others. For example:

    If you follow the traffic rules you never get back home on time; if you follow the rules for business you never make a profit; if you are always honest you never get a chance to be promoted...

    Can you see the difference? This is a common phenomenon in developing countries. So if she doesn't follow the rules in her own country, please don't assume she doesn't value laws and regulations anywhere. The truth is quite possibly the opposite, and she values them very much. China and the Chinese people are currently working hard to improve the legal system. Remember the bottom line is that she is willing to obey the laws and follow the rules in a country with an organized and equally applied legal system.

4. Education and career

    In the old days, a good education was the only road leading to a good career, and a good career (with a good income and significant power) was the only goal in life for people in China. This tradition still applies to most Chinese today. With the more competitive life in the new era, it is even more important for people to get a good education. It is very difficult for ordinary people to find a good white collar job without a university degree or above, and other ways of making a living are not easy. No good job means no future, and no future means being wanted by no one.

In the meantime there are still limited openings in Chinese universities. As of 2005, only 15% of those leaving secondary school are allowed to enter university [2]. If people fail to go to university immediately upon graduating from secondary school, it is even more difficult for them to enter higher education at a later date. The stress from the difficulty of university admission and the competition for a good job is enough to drive the Chinese people crazy at times. People have been forced to put more and more attention on academic performance. The consequences are predictable:

- Education level and career type are the important criteria in a life partner
- Education of the children is the most important thing in a parent's life
- Intensive focus and pressure are put on the children's academic study
- Rigorous study leaves no time to develop other interests

You may find your lady has some or all of the above attitudes, which may be very different from yours. If so, try to understand her point of view, and at the same time explain to her how people see things in the West:

- Level of education doesn't always reflect one's intelligence and upbringing
- There are other ways to be successful besides going to university
- Happiness is more important than education and career
- No one should think you are a loser because of your education or career.

5. Raising children

I still remember clearly the conversation that Richard had with me seven years ago:

As our dating developed, Richard and my daughter Simone were getting closer and closer. The conversation started after we had a very happy family day. That evening, after Simone went to bed, Richard raised the subject:

"Look, I have to talk about this with you. It has been in my mind since last Tuesday, when you got angry with Simone and you hit her with your hand. I felt hurt. It is probably part of your culture to treat your own children in this way. However I never see it in my family and I cannot accept it if we live together."

Richard sounded so serious that it shocked me at first, although I too was upset by what I did that day. I knew hitting children was not allowed in the West. Soon, I was touched and more relaxed because I knew Richard's concern was from his love and responsibility for Simone. I promised him that I would try not to do it again. Then I saw a big relief on Richard's face. From that moment, I knew there would be future conflicts on raising children, but I was more than happy to take the challenge for Simone's best interest.

Now Richard and I have been married for 7 years and we have our second child, Leo. We are still working on finding the best way for our children. Richard and I have adjusted to each other so well since we've been married that most of time we don't feel the cultural difference between us, except when it comes to the education of our children. Many of these differences are based on our diverse backgrounds:

In Chinese tradition:	The reason to have children is to serve you when you are old.
In the West:	The reason to have children is because you enjoy them.

In Chinese tradition:	Children have the responsibility to listen to, obey and look after parents because parents have given them their lives.
In the West:	You choose to have children; therefore you have responsibilities to bring a happy life to them.
In Chinese tradition:	Children carry out their parents' wishes and every parent wants their son or daughter to be a dragon or phoenix (ahead of others).
In the West:	Children are all individual and they live for themselves. When they grow up they can do what they want. Their happiness is the most important.
In Chinese tradition:	A proverb for parents says "hitting [physical discipline] is care and swearing [verbal discipline] is love". Criticism makes one move forward.
In the West:	It is frowned upon to hit children. Be respectful and friendly to each other. Praise and encouragement creates self esteem which allows one to move forward.

These may be summarized by a single key difference:

In Chinese tradition:	Children belong or partly belong to their parents and they live for their parents, as well as for themselves.
In the West:	Children are individuals and they live for their own happiness.

> We believe Sino-Western families can raise the best children in the world if they maintain a positive attitude in dealing with the differences. To achieve this, simply remind yourself that you both love your children, and you are both working for your children's best interest.

The cultural differences have resulted in different ways of raising children. I personally think there are advantages and disadvantages on both sides. The ideal way would be a compromise. Raising children is a challenge and something that Richard and I are still learning and exploring. In the meantime, we believe Sino-Western families can raise the best children in the world if they maintain a positive attitude in dealing with the differences. To achieve this, simply remind yourself that you both love your children, and you are both working for your children's best interest.

6. Sex and money

   These are important as well and have been covered in the last chapter. Please refer to the sections in Chapter 3.

After reading my explanations of the issues above, I hope you won't take opposing views personally without first thinking through them carefully. Now you will know that they may result from political promotion, survival needs or traditional influences in her background. I can't cover every issue here. However if you both have similar values and good communication, your relationship can survive without being an expert on the other person's background.

> To have the right attitude towards a difference is much more important than the difference itself. If someone doesn't have the right attitude, they can't make a relationship work even if they are from the same background.

When we speak of a "different background" we don't mean everything is different. Humans are humans and they all have some common sense. Don't let the differences hold you back. To have the right attitude towards a difference is much more important than the difference itself. You can learn about it, understand it, respect it, try to adapt or create a compromise, and finally be able to live with the difference. If someone doesn't have the right attitude, they can't make a relationship work even if they are from the same background.

4   Reassurance

If you are in love with her, it is important to let her know that she is always in your mind and that you love her always. It is particularly important if you don't see her in person very often, for example if you live far away, if you meet her on the Internet, or if you have to travel away for a length of time.

Our Chinese ladies often feel deeply loved, not because of the beautiful words or romantic letters that they receive, but because of the security they feel.

Yan has had unhappy experiences before, which turned her into an unbelieving person. In order to reassure her of his love, Daniel set up a camera in his house in USA. He leaves his computer connected to the Internet 24 hours a day. If Yan wants to see him, she can do so at any time, as long as he is home. If he is not home, Yan can send a message or call him on his mobile phone. In only one year, Daniel made three trips from the USA to China just to see her. Yan says: "Daniel is such a thoughtful person who has made me feel ever so secure. We are so close to each other that no one can separate us."

Dan [not the Daniel in the above example] met Hong before Christmas. From Canada, his normal country of residence, Dan went back home to England for the holidays. In case she worried, Dan gave his parents' home address and phone number to Hong so she could still reach him at any time. Dan also promised to call her every day. Hong was studying at university and didn't have her own computer. For two months, Dan called her for an hour each and every day. The calls weren't extremely romantic, but because of his actions Hong felt loved deeply.

Why is security so important to her? Because it shows your commitment. We all know that commitment is important for a relationship. Where there is no commitment, there is no relationship. Commitment means that we choose to love this person for the long term, in real life, with all its ups and downs…and we continue make that same choice every day.

Reassurance is a way to reiterate your commitment for each other and is an effective way to keep up good communication. People need more assurance in a more challenging relationship because there is a bigger demand for commitment. Please say "I love you" as many times as possible and let her know that she can always contact you, particularly when you both are going through difficulties or when she feels down.

5   Help her learn English

Although language is not the only skill necessary for good communication, it is essential. If you want your relationship to work, please help her improve her English language ability. It is truly appreciated if you learn Chinese from her, but in all practicality helping her learn English is a much quicker and more efficient way for the two of you to achieve good communication.

The Chinese language, and reading and writing in particular, are much harder to learn. Today many Westerners meet Chinese women on the Internet or keep in touch by email, so reading and writing play an important role. To be able to read and write Chinese, you need to know at least 5000 Chinese characters, while English words use only the 26 letters of the alphabet. I personally think it is impossible for an adult to learn Chinese if he is not actually in China. It is also more practical to teach her your language because sooner or later she is likely to move to your country.

Learning English is now very popular in China. Everyone realizes that English has become an international language and is a very useful skill. 80% of Chinese primary and secondary schools teach English. People who have been to college or university know, more or less, English. If people don't have a chance to learn it at school, there are many English courses and schools available on the market. In general, it is not at all difficult for Chinese to find ways to learn English. However it is still difficult for them to find ways to practice the language.

We have found dating is a very effective way for the Chinese lady to learn and practice English. You can be her best teacher. From her attitude towards learning English, you also can see how serious she is about the relationship. Our experience has shown that women who really concentrate on learning English are much more committed to the relationship than those who do not. They are also the ones who are more likely to find true love. I tell our ladies that a Western man normally doesn't mind her limited English (because he doesn't know Chinese either), as long as he can see her enthusiasm for communicating with him by working hard to learn his language.

If she is not willing to learn English, her commitment and intentions may be questionable. As noted before, there are Chinese ladies who use agents or translators to find and communicate with their dates. I am pretty confident that most of these ladies are looking for something other than true love, because true love requires direct interaction.

Be patient and encouraging as you teach her English step by step. There are many ways to help. Some men correct her written and spoken English, some tape themselves speaking and have her listen attentively, some pay for the lady to take better quality English classes (a good class with a foreign teacher is much more expensive than one with a local teacher), some give her English lessons once or twice a week themselves. Use simple words and sentence structures and speak slowly and very clearly at the beginning. Some ladies begin with the help of translation software. This is useful, but it also makes mistakes and can cause confusion or misunderstanding between the two of you. Be aware of this and give her a chance to clarify her meaning.

We all know that the most important factors in learning a new language are motivation and practice. Our experience proves that with her sincere determination and your good help, her English can be improved from a basic level of only a few words to being able to carry on an effective conversation in two to three months time. In the meantime, show an interest in learning her language. Although learning Chinese is not as easy and effective as learning English, your own determined intentions will motivate her to do her best in learning your language.

6   Choose the right communication tools

Even if you don't see her in person you still can communicate effectively if you use the right tools. Nowadays technology has brought us incredible convenience in life, and modern means of communication are one of the significant benefits. From letters to emails and from telephone to video camera or webcam, today people can send messages instantly instead of needing to wait days or weeks. People can talk and see each other even across seas and mountains. With the use of the Internet, people can feel as if their lovers are there in person no matter where they may actually be located.

Internet communication has brought people together from every corner of the world and as a result has made international dating more positive. Many cross-cultural relationships are long distance in nature, either at the beginning or at some later stage. With Internet communication, the long distance relationship ("LDR") is no longer a difficult choice—it can in fact be a good choice with a high rate of success. One of our gentlemen said:

> *"Many people are surprised by the fact I found someone outside the USA and wonder how I can maintain a relationship with someone so far away. They also don't realize she is as close as my heart and only a computer screen away and we spend three to six hours a day Seeing, Chatting, and Talking: that is more than many couples do when they live together."*

Although Internet communication is excellent and effective, it takes skill to make good use of it. Email, online chatting, voice and webcam all have their own features and advantages. Wisely using them will be a bonus to your LDR, otherwise they are useless and at worst could even let you down. For example, one person might chat online with several different women at the same time and get his messages mixed up; another might speak with her by voice before she is ready; or someone might spend too much time on the Internet and lose focus, thus turning efficiency into inefficiency.

For those who meet each other for the first time on the Internet, we suggest using email for a start. After a month of initial communication via email, you can begin using online chat and webcam if you want to further develop the relationship. By then you should have a better idea about your lady, and you can use your time and effort to concentrate only on those with real potential. Being able to focus on understanding each other's thoughts is important for a successful marriage. Internet communication can bring you great advantages in this area.

Don't talk to her by telephone too soon. As I explained before, Chinese women don't have many opportunities to practice English, particularly oral English. She will be even more nervous to try speaking English to someone who she has just met. Let her get to know you first, and then call her when she is ready. Plan your first call so it will be an exciting landmark, rather than something odd and suspicious.

Once you fall in love, use the Internet access available to communicate with each other every day. If something happens and you are not able to contact her for some time, please let her know. As people have become more spoiled by modern life, they have become less tolerant. In lovers, without advance notice, one can get into a panic if they don't hear from the other even after only one day!

Communication Tips for a
Long Distance Relationship (LDR)

1. Keep in daily communication via email

2. Reply to her emails as soon as possible

3. Phone or talk to her online via webcam once or twice a week

4. Ensure she can contact you anytime and anywhere

5. Let her know she is always on your mind

6. Share your life by telling her what is going on in your week, and listen to her as well

7. Reassure her by saying "I love you" as many times as possible, especially when you are going through difficulties

8. Remind yourself continuously that being together is more important than anything else and nothing can stop you from joining her

9. Let her know that you will overcome all difficulties to be with her

10. Send her flowers, presents or cards on her birthday and on Valentine's Day

11. Be open with her, and remove any weed between you before it grows too big

12. Talk about your plans for your future life together

13. See her in person as many times as possible (suggest two to three times a year)

14. Be honest and show trust and commitment to each other at all times

**Make good use of your LDR to achieve a solid
foundation for your love!**

References

[1] Connecting You to Love/Finding True Love Online—written by Li Xiao Yan and published by Cosmos Books (Hong Kong)/China Youth Press (Mainland China).

[2] 2005 information from www.china.org.cn

Chapter 5   *Chinese Cultural Tips on Dating and Marriage*

Language and cultural differences are two challenges of cross-cultural relationships. To some they are barriers and difficult to overcome, and to others they are exciting and not a problem at all. Whatever kind of person you are, love can make everything possible.

One of my best Chinese friends married a New Zealander. Prior to marrying my Chinese friend, this third generation Kiwi had lived alone in the same house for twenty years and was very settled in his ways. After 10 years of marriage, he still keeps some of the routines from his single life. However in the meantime, it is amazing to see him make changes little by little as their marriage progresses. It was a big effort for him, but he did it and his wife appreciates it!

Many Chinese ladies like Western cultures and are willing to learn and live with them. But some are not familiar with Western cultural traditions and need time to learn and accept them. You are in the exact same situation with regard to the Chinese culture. A healthy relationship is founded on equality and respect. Learning and accepting each other's culture is important.

While learning and accepting each other's culture, remember "when in Rome, do as the Romans do". Every culture is not always universally applicable and every culture is also not always the best. Take advantage of more than one culture—enjoy the differences, benefit from the best and discard the rest. The modern world requires us to have an open mind to enjoy its diversity. Neither my husband nor I are Scottish, but Scottish country dance has brought us together and continued to cheer us up in life.

To help you to learn and adjust to Chinese culture, I have listed the following tips on dating and marriage. Chinese cultural traditions are the product of Chinese history. If you know Chinese history or you have read chapters 1 and 2 of this book, then you will easily understand the background of these guidelines.

1. General culture tips

1. In dating, many ladies are still a little coy and would like to be chased by men rather than initiating moves themselves. If they do write to you first, please be encouraging, polite and responsive.

2. Good education means a good future in China, so be understanding if she pays more attention to one's level of education than you do (see Chapter 4).

3. Good financial status means security, which to Chinese ladies is important for the relationship. This is different than being money-minded.

4. It is acceptable to ask about people's salary, age and health. These are not seen as private matters.

5. In China divorced or widowed ladies, with or without children, have difficulty finding a new husband. Here is your chance to find a mature and charming Chinese lady!

6. If she has a good command of English, it most likely means she is well educated.

7. If she speaks little English, it doesn't necessarily mean her English is bad. It could be that she has had no chance to practice. Be patient, she will pick it up soon.

8. It is common not to have a religion in China because religion was banned during the Mao period (see Chapter 1).

9. Please let her know your dating intentions, as many ladies are still dating for marriage only (see Chapter 2).

10. She may not be so punctual, good at booking ahead or keeping to dates or appointments. Please give her a chance to learn Western ways regarding timing and planning.

11. Men are expected to pay for dinners, shows, and other expenses while on a date. Sharing the cost is too advanced for her while dating (see Chapter 3).

12. Most ladies cannot drink alcohol, therefore dinner is strongly recommended over going out for a drink, whether for social occasions or for a date.

13. Most ladies are too shy to say "I love you". They may say "I like you" instead.

14. Chinese ladies show their feelings in an elegant and indirect way. They may love you very much, but not tell you or show it on the surface.

15. Most ladies show their love by looking after you, e.g. your clothes, your food, your health, etc. This doesn't mean she wants to run your life.

16. If your girlfriend helps you tidy up your room when she visits you, or looks after you when you are sick, it means that she likes/loves you and wants to do something for you. Do not feel offended.

17. Asking about people's health and looking after them when they are unwell is one of the important ways to show concern and love.

18. If you are not sure about your intentions, do not rush to have sex with her (see Chapter 3).

19. Do not be frightened about meeting her family. In most cases, they are all very nice and friendly. Also try to learn a few simple Chinese phrases ('hello', 'thank you' and so on).

20. When you visit it is a good idea to bring some presents to her parents and young family members (ask her what is appropriate).

21. Pleasing your girlfriend's parents will make getting her to marry you much easier and her time with you happier. The best way to please them is to show you care about them as well as their daughter (e.g. asking about their health).

22. She pleases your parents to please you. To her, parents still have an important influence on your relationship (see Chapter 2).

23. It is becoming popular to share the cost of the wedding; however there may still be the traditional influence where the cost is borne mainly by the groom (see Chapter 1).

24. Highly educated Chinese ladies expect to share their thoughts with their partner, and to share housework as well (see Chapter 2).

25. As a result of the one child policy in their country, abortion is widely accepted by Chinese ladies.

26. The important days in her diary are likely to be: her birthday, Valentine's Day, Chinese New Year's Eve (the last day of the year is based on the lunar calendar), and the Moon Festival (August 15th based on the lunar calendar, the family gathering day). Please ask her about Chinese customs on these days.

27. Please let her know the important days and customs in your culture.

2. Food cultural tips

Why do I talk about "food tips" separately? It seems like a small thing compared with life goals and values, but in reality it is very important. First, you have to eat every day, and second, "food" has more meaning in both Western and Chinese cultures than just for stomach satisfaction. If you don't like or accept each other's eating manners or favorite foods, it can be a big problem in your love relationship.

I often see love hit the rocks because of food. Blue cheese vs. pickled bean curd; canned spaghetti vs. instant noodles; tomato sauce vs. soy sauce; bread vs. rice; rare steak vs. raw fish...The couples laugh at each other's choices and eat separately. Gradually it extends to personality dislikes and hurt esteem. The relationship faces real difficulties. When you are in the midst of falling in love, you can overlook the food challenge. But when the honeymoon period is over and you are living together, it will become something that you have to face every day. If you have the right attitude in dealing with it, you will enjoy the difference; otherwise it will really affect your affinity for each other and lead you to a relationship crisis.

I understand it is not easy to change the eating habits of a lifetime. It has taken me years to enjoy foods such as cheese and cream. Luckily, my British husband was very flexible and I didn't need to force myself to try Western food. But I chose to try because I knew he would miss his own food after awhile, and since he did it for me I wanted to do the same for him. Once I did try, I was surprised by the result. I am now so pleased that I made the effort because not only do I have more things in common to share with my husband, but also I am able to enjoy more varieties of food from around the world!

Give yourself a chance to try new food as long as you are not com-pletely repulsed by it (like the chicken feet or thousand year old eggs that my husband still doesn't like). You will be surprised by what you find in the end. Remember, when you try different food, you actually taste the culture behind it as well. This helps you understand each other through what you eat. It is said that the "culture of food" has played an important role in culture in general.

When my husband and I first visited his parents in the UK, the thing that made me nervous most was to have dinner with his parents. On the dining table, every one had to sit in the places as arranged by my mother-in-law, who served the food for everyone in a certain order as well. No one started to eat the food until my father-in-law began, after my mother-in-law finished serving. Those who had finished the food on their plate had to wait until my mother-in-law was ready to start the second serving. Again, without a good excuse no one could leave the table before others had finished their food. Over the dinner, talking was gentle, eating was quiet and motion was exact. Poor Simone, my nine year old daughter, was the one to suffer most from those table manners.

At home in China, table manners are not so important anymore. I grew up in a time when people struggled with limited food. Nowadays, although food is plentiful, people still treat it as the best way to show their hospitality. Food itself is much more important than the way it is eaten. Over the dining table, people share food from the same plates or bowls and offer food to each other all the way though the meal. People are talking and laughing while they eat. The whole atmosphere melts the people together through food. Eating together brings people close, which is the custom for both home and business in China.

> When you try different food, you actually taste the culture behind it as well. This helps you understand each other through what you eat. It is said that the "culture of food" has played an important role in culture in general.

Now I enjoy Western table manners that are elegant and social, as well as Chinese table manners that are friendly and close. In our family, we have a Chinese way to eat on weekdays and a Western way to eat at weekends. We enjoy the compromise. Compromise is also reflected in our respect, tolerance, understanding and effort in the relationship. To help you learn and adjust to the differences surrounding food, I have listed the following pointers:

1. Inviting people for dinner or lunch is a commonly used social and friendly custom in China, like inviting people for drinks in the West.

2. Sharing the cost of meals is not widely accepted in China. The one who suggests dinning out is the one who normally pays the bill.

3. It is common to see people rushing out or fighting their way to the cashier to pay the bill in public.

4. It is common for her parents to invite you for dinner or lunch the first time they meet you.

5. Avoid inviting yourself to visit Chinese around lunch or dinner time unless you clarify with them beforehand that you are not staying to eat.

6. The menus for lunch and dinner are similar in China, which means many Chinese pay the same attention to lunch as they do to dinner.

7. It is nice to bring something when you are invited for dinner or lunch at someone's house. However it is not customary to buy

something to share during the meal, like drinks or desserts. It is better to buy something that you can leave behind for them to enjoy later (ask your girlfriend for ideas).

8. It is polite to offer to help the host before or after the meal, even though they may not actually need help.

9. Offering food to the guest at the dining table is a traditional Chinese custom. Even though you have told them you are full, they may still offer more food to you if your plate is empty. If this is the case, I would suggest you keep some food on your plate.

10. Try to offer food to your guests if you are the host. If you don't offer food and depend on your guests to serve their own food, they may feel ignored or too shy to help themselves.

11. Talking and laughing loudly when eating is common in China. Eating helps to break the ice for new acquaintances and brings old friendships closer. Eating makes Chinese relax. Try to respect this even if you are not used to people making noises when they eat.

12. Chopsticks are the main tools for Chinese to use at meal times. It is necessary to hold the bowl up to the lips to make it easier to scoop rice or noodles into the mouth quickly and neatly.

13. If you don't know how to use chopsticks and don't want to hold up the bowl, please ask for a spoon. Chinese readily accept your ways of eating.

14. Don't feel surprised if there is still food left on the table after the meal—but don't offer to finish it. Finishing all the food on the table could imply there wasn't enough.

15. Usually, there is only one course of Chinese food. The food normally comes all together and people eat the different dishes all at the same time. People have tea or fruit instead of having coffee or desserts after the main meal.

16. It is polite to make compliments about your host's cooking and to show your appreciation.

17. Give yourself a chance to try different Chinese foods. It is easier to choose Chinese restaurants that are targeted at Westerners for a start, or try dumplings and Yum Cha (Dim Sum)*.

18. Give her time to get used to Western foods. Italian food (pasta and pizza) is an easier start for her food adventure. Indian curry is likely to be too strong and French cuisine too plain.

19. Don't try to please her by taking her to an elegant western restaurant too soon, because she may feel uneasy and not appreciate it as much as you expect.

20. Chinese people are not familiar with using a knife and fork. Don't be afraid to teach her how when you are having Western food. She is more than happy to learn.

21. If you think she spends too much time cooking (at least two dishes per meal is normal for home cooking in China), please let her know. Chinese women are inclined to show their love by focusing on making nice food for their husband.

22. Gradually create opportunities for her to try the social setting, elegance and romance of Western dining. She will discover that the environment is just as important as the food itself in the nourishment of your love.

* Yum Cha (Dim Sum) is a lunch common in Southern China comprising a wide variety of small shared dishes. Normally waitresses use carts to bring different dishes to your table for you to choose from. It is a very friendly, social, family oriented and easygoing setting.

In summary, although cultural differences may exist, with love they can be understood, accepted, compromised on, and overcome. At the beginning, you will probably notice more of the differences between you. As time passes, and as you become closer, you will notice fewer of them. Eventually you will find that she is an individual like anyone else, and you will forget that she is Chinese or Western. One of our Chinese ladies said:

"I think people are all the same in the world. Among them, there are good or bad, inward or outward, good tempered or short tempered...The point is which kind of person you are and which kind of person you match.

Communication, understanding and acceptance are important. There is no question about the challenges from cultural differences. However the barriers are caused not because of the cultural difference, but because of a wrong personality match or a lack of understanding and acceptance."

I agree. The final match is the combination of two individuals, whereas "culture" is actually practiced by each individually. So don't feel surprised if some of the cultural tips here do not apply in your case. In the end, it will be entirely up to the two of you to work through!

> The final match is the combination of two individuals, whereas "culture" is actually practiced by each individually. In the end, it will be entirely up to the two of you to work through!

Chapter 6   Getting Married—
The Paperwork

If she is living in China, there are two ways for you to marry her: Marry her in China and then apply for a visitor visa to your country, or apply for a fiancée visa and marry her in your country.

From our experience at Asian Promise, most men from Western countries other than the USA choose to marry her in China first. After the marriage, it normally takes three to six months (depending on the country) to process her visitor visa to your country. This is quicker than applying for a fiancée visa, which normally takes longer than six months. It is still difficult for mainland Chinese to obtain a visitor visa to any first world country except by joining an arranged tour group.

By contrast, most American men choose to apply for a fiancée visa first, and then get married in the USA. This is because in the USA it is quicker to process a fiancée visa (nine to twelve months) than to process her visitor visa after marriage in China (over a year). If you are working and living in China, marrying her in China would, of course, be your first choice.

Although every country has its own policy and process for marrying someone from another country, every country requires you to provide good evidence to show your love is true. Therefore please do keep all evidence such as your written correspondence (especially letters delivered through the postal service), emails, telephone bills, papers to prove your visit(s) to China, photos to prove you have been together, and how and where you met. Collecting these items from the start will let you breathe easier and help you smooth the process a great deal.

The processing of your paperwork can be a long wait for lovers. However in most cases it hasn't proven to do any harm, and in fact has often done a lot of good. It has helped people to mature their love while they wait, and to value their love even more after they marry. So far, we haven't heard of any couples married through Asian Promise who have separated or divorced. We owe this to our members' sincerity, and to the effort that they have spent prior to marrying. Be positive about it and remember that many people have taken years and years to finally find the happiness of their right match.

I have gathered here some information on paperwork to help you on your way. Please note I supply the information in good faith but don't guarantee correctness or validity. Please do contact the relevant authorities for full and updated details.

> The processing of your paperwork can be a long wait for lovers. However in most cases it hasn't proven to do any harm, and in fact has often done a lot of good.

1.   Marry her in China

The Chinese government policy for Sino-foreign marriage is controlled by the Ministry of Civil Affairs of the People's Republic of China.

> ### How to Get Married in China for Sino-Foreign Couples [1]
>
> Local marriage registration offices are the governmental bodies that are responsible for issuing marriage certificates under Chinese law for a man and woman to become husband and wife.

Step 1: Submit the Required Documents

The Sino-foreign couple must go together, in person to the local marriage registration office (where the Chinese partner has her residential registration called Hukou in Chinese) and submit:

Jointly

(1) A completed "Marriage Registration Application Form" (available at the local marriage registration office)
(2) Three photos of the marrying couple taken together
(3) A registration fee

Chinese Partner (Her)

(4) ID and the certificate of residential registration/Hukou
(5) A certificate of marital status (from her employer or local official)
(6) A health certificate (from a local hospital that is designated by the marriage registration office)

Foreign Partner (You)

(7) A current passport
(8) Chinese Visa (the documents to prove your stay in China is legal)
(9) A certificate of marital status*
(10) A health certificate (from a local hospital that is designated by the marriage registration office)

* Basically the marriage registration office needs a certificate from your home government stating you are not married in your home country. Every government has its own standard

for these certificates. Please check with your home country or your country's embassy in China. Chinese translations (translated by a notary) must accompany the certificate.

Note: The paperwork required may vary slightly from office to office. It is suggested to double check with the local marriage registration office about your paperwork, as well as about the local hospital where you need to go for the medical certificate.

Step 2: Wait for the Good News

After submitting all the papers required by the local marriage registration office, it normally only takes about one hour or so for the office to check and approve your application.

Step 3: Congratulations

Once it is approved, the marriage registration office will issue you and your partner with a marriage certificate.

Note: It will normally take some days to get the medical certificate and marriage certificate. However you can have them as quickly as the same day if you are willing to pay extra money (the cost will depend on local standards).

After you marry her in China, she can then apply for a visitor visa to see you in your country. This will take three to six months, depending on the country. The best way to find out is to make an enquiry to the relevant authority in your country.

Do your best to get everything that is possibly required for the visa processing. Her visa is usually issued by the embassy of your country in China. If the embassy doesn't have everything they need, your case could be delayed by a few weeks or a few months.

2.   Marry her in your country

Because it is difficult or sometimes impossible for mainland Chinese to obtain a visitor visa before they are married to you, a fiancée visa is probably the only way for you to marry her in your country. Every country has its own policy and process to apply for a fiancée visa, and you will need to check with the relevant authorities in your country to find out what is necessary in your situation. Since the American one is that most applied for, and since I cannot cover all the other countries, I provide here some information on applying for a fiancée visa to the USA [2]. This information is for reference only. If it differs from that provided by the U.S. Citizenship and Immigration Services ("USCIS"), please use the USCIS version.

2.1   What is a Fiancée Visa (K-1 Visa)?

The K-1 Visa, also known as the fiancée Visa, may be used by United States citizens who wish to bring their prospective husbands or wives to the United States with the intention of getting married. Minor children of the fiancée can also accompany them to the United States; they will be issued K-2 visas. The U.S. citizen must file a petition with the USCIS on behalf of the foreign fiancée. After the petition is approved, the fiancée can obtain a K-1 fiancée visa. The K-1 visa is issued at a U.S. embassy or consulate abroad. The marriage must take place within 90 days of the fiancée entering the United States.

Until the actual marriage takes place, the fiancée is considered a non-immigrant. A non-immigrant is a foreign national seeking to temporarily enter the United States for a specific purpose. A fiancée may not obtain an extension of the 90-day original non-immigrant admission. After the marriage takes place, the foreign national may apply for a "Green Card through Marriage" to become a United States citizen.

2.2   How to apply for a Fiancée Visa (K-1 Visa)

<u>Paperwork Required:</u>

1. Form I-129F: Petition for Alien Fiancée filled in by the U.S. citizen.

2. Declaration that you have met in person within the last two years.

3. Letters (from both the US Citizen and foreign fiancée) certifying an intent to marry within 90 days of entering the US on a valid K-1 Visa.

4. Proof of having met in the last two years.

5. G-325A (biographic information) filled out by the US Citizen, signed and dated.

6. One passport-type photo of the US Citizen.

7. G-325A (biographic information) filled out by the foreign fiancée, signed and dated.

8. One passport-type photo of the foreign fiancée.

9. Copy of the birth certificate for the US Citizen, or a copy of ALL pages of the US Citizen's passport issued with a validity of at least five years, or a copy of a naturalization certificate. This is used to establish citizenship.

10. Copy of the passport or birth certificate for the foreign fiancée.

11. Copy of Divorce Decree(s) or Certificate(s) for the US Citizen and/or foreign fiancée if either has been previously married.

After gathering all the paperwork required, the U.S. petitioner sends all the documents along with the I-129F to the local Service Center (location is dependent on where the petitioner lives). There are four local Service Centers at the moment: California Service Center (CSC), Nebraska Service Center (NSC), Texas Service Center (TSC) and Vermont Service Center (VSC).

The process and timeline:

The timeline below will help you visualize the entire process. It is designed to illustrate a typical K-1 Visa application process and should be used for reference only.

There are five steps in the entire process. They are called P1, P2, P3, P4 and Final Interview.

P1—The U.S. petitioner receives first Notice of Action (NOA) from USCIS acknowledging the K-1 petition has been opened and advises your case number for later reference. This normally takes two to three weeks.

P2—The U.S. petitioner receives second Notice of Action (NOA) from USCIS acknowledging the K-1 petition has been approved and your case has been forwarded by your Service Center to the National Visa Center (NVC). This takes anywhere from one to two months, to six or eight months, depending on the work load of the local Service Center.

P3—After background checks on the individuals, the NVC will forward the case to the U.S. Embassy in the city of Guangzhou (GZ), China (not far from Hong Kong), who receives and processes the package. They will send a letter and a fiancée visa application form to the fiancée (the "beneficiary"). This takes about two or three months.

P4—The beneficiary sends the completed form to GZ who will check it and enter the details into the computer system. If everything is approved, GZ will issue the beneficiary with an interview date. In the meantime, GZ will also send the beneficiary documents for a medical checkup. This step takes about two to four months depending on the GZ work load.

Interview—The beneficiary has an interview at GZ for the K-1 visa. The visa officer (an American) will make sure your love is true. All being well, the case is approved (all cases have been approved, from our experience at Asian Promise). The K-1 visa will be issued the day after the interview. It takes about one month from P4 to interview.

The current waiting time from P1 to interview is about six to twelve months. The average is about nine months. This is based on everything going smoothly and no unusual situations. Again, do your best to get everything that could possibly be required for each step of the process. Having to submit supplementary information at any step means another delay.

2.3   Do I need to use an attorney?

Regarding using an attorney to apply for a Fiancée Visa (K-1 Visa) on your behalf, one of our experienced men from Asian Promise has suggested:

> *"If a person is confident in reading up on this process and with a booklet to make sure the package has the supporting documents, and assuming the person has the spare time, I think it can be done without an attorney and the money can be saved for other usage. But, if a person is extremely busy and their time is too valuable or if they are not the type to be able to read, comprehend and follow all of the directions down to the last detail or if there are any "sticky" issues, then I think the fees for a GOOD attorney would be money well spent."*

2.4   Extra information

For people living in the USA while their lovers are in China, I recommend the websites www.candleforlove.com and www.001.com.cn/forum/usa/index.html, where you can find lots of useful information and support on your visa process and your anxious time of waiting. Most of our men and women have been members of these websites during the period of long distance dating and prior to being reunited. These are also places for people to share their happiness and difficulties.

Reference

[1]   Source: www.gov.cn, www.ebeijing.gov.cn

[2]   Source: www.usimmigrationsupport.org/visa_k1.html,
      www.visajourney.com/forums/index.php?autocom=custom&page=k1guide,
      www.shusterman.com

Afterword

It took me only four months to write this book, which is as fast as I wrote my book for Chinese ladies [1]. What I have written has actually been in my mind for a long time. I just needed to put it into writing. I enjoyed the writing process and I am pleased to finally see my thoughts became words. I have to say they were burning so strongly in my mind that I was worried they might vanish one day if I didn't let them out.

It is great to see my book has already interested so many people. Ten copies of the e-book were sold before it was even completed, and people were desperate to read the rest of it. I joked with my husband that I had broken a world record—selling a book to readers before its completion! However it is far more than a joke. It has made me think seriously about why there weren't any books on the market to meet this clear need. Well, there certainly are books for dating Asian ladies, but they are mostly for fun and play. Does that mean Westerners are not interested in dating Chinese/Asians for true love and serious relationships? Absolutely not!

I have received some feedback from readers. Most have told me the book is fascinating, while some including my husband, think it is very useful and enlightening. I liken this difference to shopping at a DIY store. If you are just a curious newcomer to home improvement, you will find it very interesting to have a look around the store. However the deeper you are in the midst of an actual project, and the stronger your urge to find the right methods to master it, the better you will understand the way the tools and materials are really used. I wish that all readers will eventually find this not only an interesting book, but also a useful book. It provides direction for beginners, wisdom for lovers and nourishment for couples.

My conclusion to the book is this: For a cross-cultural relationship, the difference is not the issue; rather it is the attitude to the difference which is the issue. If you are a person who likes difference and challenge, then a cross-cultural relationship is a Godsend. However, the heart of the issue is "LOVE". With love, everything is possible!

Life without love is dark, and life without challenge is dull. I wish that all of you will enjoy your life, and find the love of your dreams in this colorful world!

Dawn Xiao Yan Li

July 2006
New Zealand

Reference

[1]   Connecting You to Love/Finding True Love Online—written by Li Xiao Yan and published by Cosmos Books (Hong Kong)/China Youth Press (Mainland China).

About the Author

Dawn Xiao Yan Li graduated with a medical degree from Beijing Medical University, China in 1983. She emigrated to New Zealand in 1991. In early 1997, Xiao Yan left New Zealand for Hong Kong to work in an international medical publisher as a senior editor. In 1999, Xiao Yan left the publisher and set up Asian Promise with her British husband Richard Kaser.

Asian Promise is a dating website that helps Chinese ladies to find love and marriage internationally. Since its launch, it has served thousands of members and has helped hundreds of people find love and marriage. From the first day of Asian Promise till now, Xiao Yan has focused all her attention on it. She has counseled many Chinese ladies and Western men on personal matters of love and relationships on a daily basis through emails and telephone calls, and annual seminars in China.

Xiao Yan moved back to New Zealand with her family in 2003. However she still goes to China every year. In her annual seminars in China, she teaches her customers to find true love and introduces Western thoughts about love and marriage to them.

In 2004, Xiao Yan put her valuable experience from Asian Promise and her own cross cultural relationships into a book for Chinese readers. It was published in Hong Kong entitled "Connecting You to Love" (in traditional characters) by Cosmos Books HK in May 2005 and in mainland China entitled "Finding True Love Online" (in simplified characters) by China Youth Press in February 2006. The book helps Chinese reform/improve the old traditions through innovation of Internet dating, as well as helping Chinese correctly understand the Western attitudes on love and marriage.

In late 2005, Xiao Yan completed her second book for Chinese readers. The book helps Chinese to achieve a happy marriage through a modern approach. It has been published as an e-book by Asian Promise Ltd. and some of the contents have been published periodically in "Marriage and Family", a famous Chinese magazine in China and owned by the All-China Women's Federation. In the meantime, Xiao Yan has become a regular column writer for "Marriage and Family".

Xiao Yan believes love is not constrained by national boarders, but love needs understanding. Building the love bridge between the East and West has always been one of the goals of Xiao Yan's work. She now aims to use her unique perspective to help Westerners to understand Chinese women and their attitudes to love. In her book "Chinese Women in Love and Marriage" Xiao Yan has illustrated Chinese women today through their past and used lots of true stories to demonstrate her views and guidelines for Western men, who want to achieve successful cross-cultural relationships with Chinese ladies. "Chinese Women in Love and Marriage" is a practical guide for Western men, as well as a useful reference book for Chinese study.

In her spare time, Dawn Xiao Yan likes reading, writing and chatting with people. However the most enjoyable things for Dawn are spending time with her family and Scottish Country Dance!

Author's Notes

1. To maintain privacy, some of the names of the people mentioned in this book have been changed.

2. The cover photo is of one of the couples from Asian Promise. The author very much appreciates their kind permission for its use.

Resources

1. If you want to find a way to meet sincere Chinese ladies for love and marriage, please go to the website: www.asianpromise.com

2. If you want to have an e-book format of this book, please go to the web page: http://www.asianpromise.com

3. If you want to obtain the book "Connecting You to Love/Finding True Love Online" mentioned in this book for your Chinese lover, please contact Dawn at love@asianpromise.com.

978-0-595-41506-9
0-595-41506-7